Literacy
in the
Science Classroom

Millie Blandford

IncentivePublications

BY WORLD BOOK
a Scott Fetzer company

Literacy in the Science Classroom

Print Edition ISBN 978-1-62950-295-3
E-book Edition ISBN 978-1-62950-296-0 (PDF)

World Book, Inc.
233 North Michigan Avenue
Suite 2000
Chicago, Illinois 60601
U.S.A.

For information about World Book and Incentive Publications products, call **1-800-967-5325,** or visit our websites at **www.worldbook.com** and **www.incentivepublications.com.**

Printed in the United States of America by Sheridan Books, Inc.
Chelsea, Michigan
1st Printing March 2015

Contents

Chapter 3 Mathematics Literacy Strategies 86

TO THINK LIKE A SCIENTIST

If our students are to think and operate like scientists, we must teach them to read, speak, discuss, listen, research, and write like scientists. Science instruction goes far beyond such knowledge-level tasks as identifying symbols for the elements, naming the classes of vertebrates, reciting Newton's laws of motion, listing the four kinds of chemical bases in DNA, or writing the chemical formula for sulfuric acid. Yes, we want students to access content! But we want them to do it in ways that nurture critical thinking, deep understanding, and relevant connections to issues and situations in the real world. Students cannot develop these skills unless they are exposed to purposeful science literacy strategies in the classroom.

About This Book

Literacy in the Science Classroom is based on the beliefs that:

- Students learn best when teachers offer engaging, stimulating, and active classroom experiences.

- Good science instruction includes a variety of hands-on strategies in a variety of formats for a variety of learners.

- Students need explicit instruction in and modeling of the skills and strategies of science literacy.

- Students must encounter reading, writing, listening, and speaking material beyond the textbooks—extending to websites, journals, newscasts, current events, videos, speeches, interviews, graphics, models, and multimedia presentations.

- In every science classroom, students need multiple opportunities to read, write, listen, investigate, research, ask questions, analyze, evaluate, collaborate and cooperate, discuss, debate, reflect, keep records, and communicate as they explore science texts, concepts, and presentations.

- After any learning experience, students should have time and ways to review, reflect on, share, and extend what they have learned.

- Students, particularly at the middle and high school levels, should gradually assume greater responsibility for their own learning.

The strategies suggested in this book are designed to put these principles into practice to increase science literacy. Strategies include dynamic science vocabulary games, inviting science learning stations, and math literacy tools that take away the dread of reading and using tricky scientific formulas.

With all the activity options in this book, students have plenty of chances to engage in the practices above. As they put these options to use, students will work with other students, increase independence, and review, reflect on, and share what they've learned. In addition to more spirited involvement in science class, you'll watch your students . . .

- increase scientific vocabulary and use it more frequently (and accurately) in conversations and writing;
- improve fluency in reading scientific literature;
- blossom in their comprehension of scientific texts;
- tackle science-math word problems with more confidence; and
- "get" and appreciate broader applications of science concepts.

How to Use This Book

Read the introduction to the chapter.
Each chapter includes a detailed introduction that describes the strategies, tells how to use them, adds ideas for differentiating learning, and informs teachers how to connect the activities to technology and to curriculum standards.

Review and choose strategies.
Choose games, stations, or math literacy strategies that fit your class and your student. Vary the games, mixing your use of whole-group and small-group games. Vary the stations, combining a variety of approaches to reach all your learners. Read the instructions for set-up and the steps for each game, station, or strategy process. Decide if you'll use the activity to introduce, teach, deepen and reinforce comprehension of, or assess mastery of science material.

Plug in your content.
Most of the activities are not content-specific. Instead, they are presented as templates or flexible guidelines that can be used with any content. This means you can tailor them to your curriculum and use the games, stations, and strategies again and again. You can even use many of them with content other than science!

Deepen or expand the activity.
Make use of the reproducible student pages where learners can record, summarize, reflect on, review, or share the concepts and results of their work. In addition, follow the suggestions accompanying many of the strategies for alternative approaches, follow-up activities, technology connections, and coverage of additional standards.

Build the language of science every day.
Pages 111 through 124 offer hundreds of science terms to expand the science vocabulary of middle and high school students. Start with the general terminology list on page 112. This is the working vocabulary that reaches into all science topics and fields. When students know, understand, and can apply these terms, they'll have a strong background for reading science materials and following directions for science tasks. Then choose terms that fit the topics and concepts your students will study. Make a copy of the lists and highlight the terms that students master as the year goes along. Students will delight in seeing the blossoming of their abilities to "speak science." For help in mastering the terms, direct the students to reliable general and specialized dictionaries and encyclopedias in the classroom, school library, or local public library. (If your school or public library subscribes to *World Book® Discover*, *World Book Student*, or other *World Book Web* publications, show your students how to use the embedded dictionary and double-click definition-retrieval function.)

Technology Twists

Technology and science have long been paired together. It's a logical, sensible, and wonderful pairing! In the pursuit of improved science literacy, take every opportunity to bring technology into the science conversations in your classroom. Likewise, find ways to mix science learning activities with technological tools and programs available in your school and classroom. You can use technology to spark interest in a topic, build background knowledge, teach a lesson, reinforce a concept, carry out an investigation, record data, carry out assessments, and much, much more.

Use this checklist to keep ideas for technology integration flowing in your classroom.

Use these tools:

____ cell phones and other smart devices

____ MP3 players or other portable music devices

____ safe social media sites and message apps

____ audio recorders

____ video cameras

____ video games

____ digital cameras

____ digital whiteboards

____ keyboards

____ video clips

_____ music recordings

_____ clickers

_____ probes

_____ computers

_____ calculators

_____ projectors

_____ Internet articles, news, and speeches

_____ Internet video clips

_____ email

Help students find and use online programs or digital apps where they can:

_____ find help with math or science tutoring, homework, or projects

_____ access reference materials

_____ create and solve math problems

_____ display statistics

_____ manipulate formulas and other equations

_____ create and manipulate linear graphs

_____ participate in or create virtual science labs

_____ watch visual demonstrations

_____ make movies and screen casts

_____ use virtual manipulatives for math or science processes (visit Utah State University's National Library of Virtual Manipulatives: http://nlvm.usu.edu/en/nav/vlibrary.html)

_____ contribute to websites, blogs and wikis

_____ download speeches and performances

_____ follow inquiry steps in virtual labs

_____ produce, save, and share audio files

_____ make posters

_____ display questions, projects, and products

_____ conduct conversations with experts

_____ build e-portfolios

_____ manipulate geometrical figures

_____ build virtual models

_____ design graphics

_____ communicate with other classes or other authentic audiences

_____ take virtual field trips

_____ learn about weather in real time

_____ view space objects through telescopes

_____ graph results of experiments

_____ design, give, and evaluate surveys

_____ use online templates to create game shows or crossword puzzles

_____ design or complete graphic organizers, timelines, puzzles, game shows,

_____ write, edit, and publish (sites such as Google Drive™, Zoho Writer™, and Issuu™)

_____ collaborate on written projects

_____ create multimedia presentations (e.g., Keynote®, PowerPoint®, Prezi™, Haiku Deck®, SlideShare™, and Google Presentations™)

Support for Literacy and Content Standards in Science and Math

As students engage in the practices of science literacy offered in this book, they'll use the **same skills** of deep reading, finding evidence, using vocabulary, analyzing the craft and structure of texts, integrating ideas, producing coherent writing, using technology to produce and present knowledge, collaborating, and presenting **that they encounter in a language arts class.** The strategies in each chapter provide support for teaching and learning content and skills of any literacy standards—be they Common Core State Standards or the college- and career-readiness literacy guidelines that make up other states' academic standards. In addition, once you add your specific content to any of these activities, you'll be strengthening related content and cross-cutting standards within the Next Generation Science Standards or other science and math standards models you follow.

Pages 10 through 16 provide charts that show where the games, stations, and strategies support the grades 6-12 Common Core Standards for Literacy in Science and Technical Subjects, Common Core Anchor Standards for Speaking and Listening, Common Core State Standards for Mathematical Practice, and Next Generation Science and Engineering Practices Standards.

Standards Connections
CCSS English Language Arts Standards
Literacy in Science & Technical Subjects, Grades 6-12

Standard Number	Standard	Connections
Key Ideas and Details		
RST.6-12.1	Cite specific textual evidence to support analysis of science and technical texts (gr 6-8), attending to the precise details of explanations or descriptions (gr 9-10), and attending to important distinctions the author makes and to any gaps or inconsistencies in the account (gr 11-12).	Ch 1 Game 8 Ch 2 Stations 1-12
RST.6-12.2	Determine the central ideas or conclusions of a text; provide an accurate summary of the text distinct from prior knowledge or opinions (gr 6-8), trace the text's explanation or depiction of a complex process, phenomenon, or concept; provide an accurate summary of the text (gr 9-10); summarize complex concepts, processes, or information presented in a text by paraphrasing them in simpler but still accurate terms (gr 11-12).	Ch 1 Games 1-10 Ch 2 Stations 1-12 Ch 3 Strategies 1-15
RST.6-12.3	Follow precisely a multistep procedure when carrying out experiments, taking measurements, or performing technical tasks (gr 6-8), attending to special cases or exceptions defined in the text (gr 9-10); analyze the specific results based on explanations in the text (gr 11-12).	Ch 1 Games 1-10 Ch 2 Stations 1-12 Ch 3 Strategies 1-15
Craft and Structure		
RST.6-12.4	Determine the meaning of symbols, key terms, and other domain-specific words and phrases as they are used in a specific scientific or technical context relevant to grades 6-12 texts and topics.	Ch 1 Games 1-10 Ch 2 Stations 1-12 Ch 3 Strategies 1-15
RST.6-12.5	Analyze the structure an author uses to organize a text, including how the major sections contribute to the whole and to an understanding of the topic (gr 6-8); analyze the structure of the relationships among concepts in a text, including relationships among key terms (gr 9-10); analyze how the text structures information or ideas into categories or hierarchies, demonstrating understanding of the information or ideas (gr 11-12).	Ch 1 Games 3-10 Ch 2 Stations 1-13 Ch 3 Strategies 1-15
RST.6-12.6	Analyze the author's purpose in providing an explanation, describing a procedure, or discussing an experiment in a text (gr 6-8), defining the question the author seeks to address (gr 9-10), identifying important issues that remain unresolved (gr 11-12).	Ch 1 Games 7, 8, 9 Ch 2 Stations 6, 7, 8 Ch 3 Strategies 1-15

Standard Number	Standard	Connections
Integration of Knowledge and Ideas		
RST.6-12.7	Integrate quantitative or technical information expressed in words in a text with a version of that information expressed visually (e.g., in a flowchart, diagram, model, graph, or table) (gr 6-8); translate quantitative or technical information expressed in words in a text into visual form (e.g., a table or chart) and translate information expressed visually or mathematically (e.g., in an equation) into words (gr 9-10); integrate and evaluate multiple sources of information presented in diverse formats and media (e.g., quantitative data, video, multimedia) in order to address a question or solve a problem (gr 11-12).	Ch 1 Games 2, 5, 6, 7, 9 Ch 2 Stations 1, 2, 3, 5, 8, 9, 13, 10, 12 Ch 3 Strategies 1-15
RST.6-12.8	Distinguish among facts, reasoned judgment based on research findings, and speculation in a text (gr 6-8); assess the extent to which the reasoning and evidence in a text support the author's claim or a recommendation for solving a scientific or technical problem (gr 9-10); evaluate the hypotheses, data, analysis, and conclusions in a science or technical text, verifying the data when possible and corroborating or challenging conclusions with other sources of information (gr 11-12).	Ch 1 Games 7, 8 Ch 2 Stations 1-15
RST.6-12.9	Compare and contrast the information gained from experiments, simulations, video, or multimedia sources with that gained from reading a text on the same topic (gr 6-8); compare and contrast findings presented in a text to those from other sources (including their own experiments), noting when the findings support or contradict previous explanations or accounts (gr 9-10); synthesize information from a range of sources (e.g., texts, experiments, simulations) into a coherent understanding of a process, phenomenon, or concept, resolving conflicting information when possible (gr 11-12).	Ch 1 Game 9 Ch 2 Stations 1, 2, 5, 6, 7, 8, 9
Range of Reading and Level of Text Complexity		
RST.6-12.10	By the end of the appropriate grade (8, 10, or 12), read and comprehend science/technical texts in the grades 6-8 (or 9-10, or 11-12) text band complexity band independently and proficiently.	Ch 1 Games 1-10 Ch 2 Stations 1-12 Ch 3 Review Lessons A-C Ch 3 Strategies 1-15

CCSS English Language Arts Standards

Writing/Literacy in History/Social Studies, Science, & Technical Subjects, Grades 6-12

Standard Number	Standard	Connections
Text Types and Purposes		
WHST.6-12.1	Write arguments focused on discipline-specific content.	Ch 2 Station 3
WHST.6-12.2	Write informative/explanatory texts, including scientific procedures/experiments and technical processes.	Ch 1 Games 1-10 Ch 2 Stations 1, 2, 3, 5, 6, 7, 8, 10
Production and Distribution of Writing		
WHST.6-12.4	Produce clear and coherent writing in which the development, organization, and style are appropriate to task, purpose, and audience.	Ch 1 Games 1-9 Ch 2 Stations 1-12 Ch 3 Strategies 1-15
WHST.6-12.6	Use technology, including the Internet, to produce and publish writing and present the relationships between information and ideas clearly and efficiently (gr 6-8). Use technology, including the Internet, to produce, publish, and update individual or shared writing products, including new arguments or information, taking advantage of technology's capacity to link to other information and to display information flexibly and dynamically (gr 9-12).	Ch 1 Games 6, 9 Ch 2 Stations 3, 5, 6, 7, 8, 9
Research to Build and Present Knowledge		
WHST.6-12.7	Conduct short research projects to answer a question (including a self-generated question), drawing on several sources and generating additional related, focused questions that allow for multiple avenues of exploration (gr 6-8). Conduct short as well as more sustained research projects to answer a question (including a self-generated question) or solve a problem; narrow or broaden the inquiry when appropriate; synthesize multiple sources on the subject, demonstrating understanding of the subject under investigation (gr 9-12).	Ch 1 Games 2, 3, 6, 8, 9 Ch 2 Stations 4, 5, 6, 7, 8, 9 Ch 3 Strategies 1-15

Standard Number	Standard	Connections
WHST.6-12.8	Gather relevant information from multiple print and digital sources, using search terms effectively; assess the usefulness, credibility and accuracy of each source in answering the research question; integrate information into the text selectively to maintain the flow of ideas, quote or paraphrase the data and conclusions of others while avoiding plagiarism and following a standard format for citation.	Ch 1 Games 2, 5, 6, 8, 9 Ch 2 Stations 3, 5, 6, 7, 8, 9, 10
WHST.6-12.9	Draw evidence from informational texts to support analysis, reflection, and research.	Ch 1 Games 7, 9 Ch 2 Stations 3, 5, 6, 7, 8, 9, 12
Range of Writing		
WHST.6-12.10	Write routinely over extended time frames (time for research, reflection, and revision) and shorter time frames (a single sitting or a day or two) for a range of discipline-specific tasks, purposes, and audiences.	Ch 1 Games 2, 3, 4, 5, 6, 7, 9 Ch 2 Stations 1-12 Ch 3 Strategies 1-15

CCSS College and Career Readiness Anchor Standards for Speaking and Listening, Grades 6-12

Anchor Standard	Standard	Connections
Comprehension and Collaboration		
CCRA.SL.1	Prepare for and participate effectively in a range of conversations and collaborations with diverse partners, building on others' ideas and expressing their own clearly and persuasively.	Ch 1 Games 1-10 Ch 2 Stations 1-12 Ch 3 Strategies 1-15
CCRA.SL.2	Integrate and evaluate information presented in diverse media and formats, including visually, quantitatively, and orally.	Ch 1 Games 6, 9, 10 Ch 2 Stations 1-12 Ch 3 Strategies 1-15
CCRA.SL.3	Evaluate a speaker's point of view, reasoning, and use of evidence and rhetoric.	Ch 2 Stations 3, 6, 8,
Presentation of Knowledge and Ideas		
CCRA.SL.4	Present information, findings, and supporting evidence such that listeners can follow the line of reasoning and the organization, development, and style are appropriate to task, purpose, and audience.	Ch 1 Games 1-10 Ch 2 Stations 1-12
CCRA.SL.5	Make strategic use of digital media and visual displays of data to express information and enhance understanding of presentations.	Ch 1 Games 6, 9 Ch 2 Stations 1, 2, 3, 5, 6, 8, 9
CCRA.SL.6	Adapt speech to a variety of contexts and communicative tasks, demonstrating command of formal English when indicated or appropriate.	Ch 1 Games 1-10 Ch 2 Stations 1-12 Ch 3 Strategies 1-15

Next Generation Science Standards
Science & Engineering Practices, Grades 6-12

Standard Number	Standard	Connections
1	Asking questions and defining problems	Ch 1 Games 7, 9, 10 Ch 2 Stations 4, 5, 6, 7, 8, 9, 10, 11 Ch 3 Strategies 1-15
2	Developing and using models	Ch 2 Stations 1, 2, 4, Ch 3 Strategies 1-15
3	Planning and carrying out investigations	Ch 2 Stations 3, 4, 9, 11, 12
4	Analyzing and interpreting data	Ch 1 Games 1-10 Ch 2 Stations 3, 9
5	Using mathematics and computational thinking	Ch 2 Station 11 Ch 3 Strategies 1-15
6	Constructing explanations and designing solutions	Ch 1 Games 1, 7, 8, 9 Ch 2 Stations 3, 4, 8, 9, 10, 11, 12 Ch 3 Strategies 1-15
7	Engaging in argument from evidence	Ch 2 Stations 4, 5, 9
8	Obtaining, evaluating, and communicating information	Ch 1 Games 1-10 Ch 2 Stations 1-12

Note: Chapter III Strategies 1-15 also support Next Generation Science Standards Disciplinary Core Ideas at the middle and high school levels:

PS2A Forces and Motion

PS3A Definitions of Energy

PS3B Conservation of Energy and Energy Transfer

PS3C Relationship Between Energy and Forces

PS4C Wave Properties

Common Core State Standards for Mathematics

Standards for Mathematical Practice, Grades 6-12

Standard Number	Standard	Connections
MP1	Make sense of problems and persevere in solving them.	Ch 2 Stations 4, 11 Ch 3 Strategies 1-15
MP2	Reason abstractly and quantitatively.	Ch 2 Station 11 Ch 3 Strategies 1-15
MP3	Construct viable arguments and critique the reasoning of others.	Ch 2 Station 11 Ch 3 Strategies 1-15
MP4	Model with mathematics.	Ch 2 Stations 4, 11 Ch 3 Strategies 1-15
MP5	Use appropriate tools strategically.	Ch 2 Stations 4, 11 Ch 3 Strategies 1-15
MP6	Attend to precision.	Ch 2 Stations 1-12 Ch 3 Strategies 1-15
MP7	Look for and make use of structure.	Ch 2 Stations 1-12 Ch 3 Strategies 1-15
MP8	Look for and express regularity in repeated reasoning.	Ch 2 Station 11 Ch 3 Strategies 1-15

Chapter 1
Science Vocabulary Games

Vocabulary is at the heart of learning, reading, writing, and understanding the language of science. In science classrooms, students will learn literally thousands of new words and phrases. They need to

- connect these terms to previously learned concepts, facts, and words;
- understand the terms when they encounter them in any text or presentation; and
- explore and expand meanings of terms within the context of the science topic, discussion, or experience.

Students will benefit from multiple contacts with science terms and multiple occasions to use them in different situations. The vocabulary games in this chapter invite students to actively engage with science terms and the concepts they represent. The games **can be adapted to any terms** and used to

- introduce students to new terminology within the context of a unit of study or a written, spoken, or visual presentation;
- strengthen and apply understandings of terminology as students work with a science topic; or
- review or assess understanding and application of terms.

Vocabulary Cards

Most of the games use vocabulary cards. Create these cards from large index cards or poster board. (For most of the games, students can create the cards.) When a game requires terms or definitions to be displayed on a big surface, make sure that the written words are large enough to be easily seen by students from anywhere in the classroom.

Group Sizes for Games

At the beginning of the description for each game, a group size is recommended. Games are designed for the whole class (labeled **Whole Class**), teams of about five students playing at the same time (labeled **Teams**), or individual small groups playing without competing against any other groups (labeled **Individual Small Groups**).

Scoring Guides and Reference Sheets

Scoring guides or other student reference sheets accompany most of the games. These templates work with vocabulary from any science lesson, topic, or unit. This means that the games can be played again and again—to teach or reinforce vocabulary and understanding of concepts in every strand of science. After the game, students can use the completed score sheets or reference sheets for study guides. Be sure to check these for accuracy before students use them for further review.

Earning Points

In all the games, there are opportunities for students to earn points. Students will be more motivated to participate and more engaged in the activities if they see a purpose for these points. Allow the points to accumulate for small prizes or privileges, or for extra-credit points on students' grades or assessments.

Winning and Losing

No matter who accumulates the most points in a round or in a game, all students are winners, because all of them can collect points. In addition, everyone wins because they end up with better understanding of science terms, concepts, and processes—particularly if the game or after-game activities include application of the terminology.

Variations: Beyond the Definitions

Some of the games offer a variation that involves students at a greater level of complexity with the concepts behind the terms. These variations are offered where the initial form of the game focuses on knowledge or comprehension levels of thinking; these will push students to higher levels of thinking, such as application, analysis, synthesis, or evaluation.

After the Game

To remember a new vocabulary term and incorporate it into his or her vocabulary, a person needs to see it used, hear it, and use it many times in several ways over a period of time. This feature offers a way for students to further engage with, reinforce, or apply their understanding of the science terminology. These tasks can be done any time after the game—including several days or weeks later.

Differentiating the Games

As you get ready for any of these games, consider the many different learners who will participate. Always offer options that will embrace varied styles, gifts, abilities, areas of struggle, speeds, comfort levels, and needs. Here are a few suggestions for differentiating learning during the games.

- Offer instructions in more than one modality; as often as possible, give oral or visual steps (or rules) along with written directions. Make sure those directions are available throughout the game for students to review as needed.

- Always have reference materials in print or on devices available for students who need to refresh their memories about terms. Supply materials at lower-than-grade-level difficulty for struggling readers.

- Group students with like talents on one team; give that team a different task with the same terms and within the same rules of the game.

- Group students with different strengths on one team; adjust the rules of the game so that multiple approaches and kinds of answers are acceptable. Different students will see different facets of a term. All students will come away from the game with greater awareness of the complexity of concepts.

- Vary the kinds of tasks within the games. For example, include demonstrating, speaking, listening, drawing, reading, and writing to give all learners chances to excel.

- Pair a struggling reader or writer with a partner who can transcribe the ideas for the duo.

- Find a way to adapt the game tasks for learners who need more time.

- To challenge students, include extra terms without supplying definitions. Students will have to use whatever resources they can to confirm word meanings.

- Include some games that allow for students to follow their own ideas and show something of an individual accomplishment—instead of or in addition to the team effort.

Connecting to Technology

- Use available technology often to enhance the games. Students can search for explanations or uses of terms on computers, tablets, or smart phones. They can share what they've learned about a term and related concept on social media sites, in podcasts, or on blogs. They can use online apps or software to create graphic organizers, posters, video clips, or comic strips to elaborate on the meanings and uses of a term.

- Several of the games include suggestions for using technology. In addition, see the section "Technology Twists" in the introduction to this book. This provides a checklist of further suggestions for integrating technology into science literacy activities (pages 7 through 9).

Connecting to Standards

Keep your standards for science content and science literacy available at all times. As you plan each game, identify standards that will be addressed through the game. Of course, it will be natural to focus on the standards that are explicitly about vocabulary. (Note that science vocabulary will include symbols, formulas, and names of big ideas [e.g., *form and function*] and processes [e.g., *controlling variables*].) But don't overlook the reading and writing standards that are also used as the game is played. Most of the games will require finding evidence in texts, drawing conclusions and making reasoned judgments, following written directions, examining relationships among terms, synthesizing information, producing clear and coherent writing, and using a number of listening and speaking skills. The Standards-Connections charts on pages 10 through 16 identify Common Core State Standards and Next Generation Science Standards practices that are addressed by the general approach of each game. However, the content and specific terminology you choose will undoubtedly add other standards to the list for that game.

GAME #1 Meaning Match-up

Whole Class

Game Objective: Continue rounds of matching until all class members are successful in matching words with their meanings.

Supplies:
- Collection of science terms (including symbols and formulas) on a topic or concept
- Cards for terms and definitions (on separate cards)
- Markers
- Copy of MEANING MATCH-UP Score Sheet for each student (copied on two sides of one sheet) (page 23)
- Tape or other substance for posting cards

Set -up:

1. Write science terms on one set of cards or strips.

2. Write definitions on another set of cards or strips.
   Note the variation on page 22.

3. Post terms with a number written beside each one.

4. Post definitions with a letter written beside each.

5. Put words and definitions in random order in places where they can be seen by all students.

Directions for MEANING MATCH-UP:

1. Students take turns reading the words and their meanings aloud, so that all students have been exposed to all the words.

2. Students match the words with the correct definitions on their score sheets in the allotted time. They do this by writing the matching number and letter (e.g., 1D, 2F). Allow about 10 minutes for the first round.

3. When the time is up, students switch papers to check each other's score sheets by putting a check mark over the correct matches. Have the students add up the checks and write the number at the bottom of the column after each round.

4. When a term is correctly matched with its meaning by every student, take the two cards down and display them in another part of the room. (Verify the correct match with the teacher or reliable reference source.)

Continued on next page.

5. Give students a few minutes to check word definitions between rounds.

6. If some of the matches are eliminated in the first round, decrease the amount of time for the second round. (Otherwise, stay with 10 minutes.)

7. Continue the game until all matches have been made, and all cards are moved.

8. Students can tally points from every round and compare the numbers of points. If you choose to identify winners, there can be an overall winner for the most points, and another set of winners for the rounds.

*Variation: Beyond the Definitions

Instead of definitions, write ***examples*** of the terms on the second set of cards. This takes the students to deeper level of understanding about the concepts connected to the terms. They'll need to have a good grasp of the definitions in order to make the leap to recognize examples of the term or concept in action!

Examples: For the term *symbiosis*, the second card might read, *A hermit crab moves into an empty seashell*, or *Mosquitoes feed on blood from other animals*. For the term *endothermic*, the second card might read, *Sweat evaporates from the skin and takes heat away from the body*, or *In photosynthesis, a plant converts light energy from the sun into sugar and other organic compounds*.

After the game:

Match students in pairs. Ask each pair to choose two or more terms that would be used in explaining a science concept. Give each pair five to 10 minutes to summarize or explain the concept, using all the chosen terms. They then pass the summary on to other students or friends in a tweet, text, or email.

GAME #1

MEANING MATCH-UP Score Sheet

Student Name _____ **Topic** _____

Round 1	Round 2	Round 3	Round 4	Round 5	Round 6	Round 7	Round 8	Round 9	Round 10
1.	1.	1.	1.	1.	1.	1.	1.	1.	1.
2.	2.	2.	2.	2.	2.	2.	2.	2.	2.
3.	3.	3.	3.	3.	3.	3.	3.	3.	3.
4.	4.	4.	4.	4.	4.	4.	4.	4.	4.
5.	5.	5.	5.	5.	5.	5.	5.	5.	5.
6.	6.	6.	6.	6.	6.	6.	6.	6.	6.
7.	7.	7.	7.	7.	7.	7.	7.	7.	7.
8.	8.	8.	8.	8.	8.	8.	8.	8.	8.
9.	9.	9.	9.	9.	9.	9.	9.	9.	9.
10.	10.	10.	10.	10.	10.	10.	10.	10.	10.
11.	11.	11.	11.	11.	11.	11.	11.	11.	11.
12.	12.	12.	12.	12.	12.	12.	12.	12.	12.
13.	13.	13.	13.	13.	13.	13.	13.	13.	13.
14.	14.	14.	14.	14.	14.	14.	14.	14.	14.
15.	15.	15.	15.	15.	15.	15.	15.	15.	15.
16.	16.	16.	16.	16.	16.	16.	16.	16.	16.
17.	17.	17.	17.	17.	17.	17.	17.	17.	17.
18.	18.	18.	18.	18.	18.	18.	18.	18.	18.
19.	19.	19.	19.	19.	19.	19.	19.	19.	19.
20.	20.	20.	20.	20.	20.	20.	20.	20.	20.

Continued on next page.

Round 1	Round 2	Round 3	Round 4	Round 5	Round 6	Round 7	Round 8	Round 9	Round 10
21.	21.	21.	21.	21.	21.	21.	21.	21.	21.
22.	22.	22.	22.	22.	22.	22.	22.	22.	22.
23.	23.	23.	23.	23.	23.	23.	23.	23.	23.
24.	24.	24.	24.	24.	24.	24.	24.	24.	24.
25.	25.	25.	25.	25.	25.	25.	25.	25.	25.
26.	26.	26.	26.	26.	26.	26.	26.	26.	26.
27.	27.	27.	27.	27.	27.	27.	27.	27.	27.
28.	28.	28.	28.	28.	28.	28.	28.	28.	28.
29.	29.	29.	29.	29.	29.	29.	29.	29.	29.
30.	30.	30.	30.	30.	30.	30.	30.	30.	30.
31.	31.	31.	31.	31.	31.	31.	31.	31.	31.
32.	32.	32.	32.	32.	32.	32.	32.	32.	32.
33.	33.	33.	33.	33.	33.	33.	33.	33.	33.
34.	34.	34.	34.	34.	34.	34.	34.	34.	34.
35.	35.	35.	35.	35.	35.	35.	35.	35.	35.
36.	36.	36.	36.	36.	36.	36.	36.	36.	36.
37.	37.	37.	37.	37.	37.	37.	37.	37.	37.
38.	38.	38.	38.	38.	38.	38.	38.	38.	38.
39.	39.	39.	39.	39.	39.	39.	39.	39.	39.
40.	40.	40.	40.	40.	40.	40.	40.	40.	40.
Total	Total	Total	Total	Total	Total	Total	Total	Total	Total

Total of all rounds _____

GAME #2 *The Last Word* **Individual Small Group**

Game Objective: Individuals try to collect the most matches by the end of the game.

Supplies:

- Collection of science terms (including symbols and formulas) on one topic or multiple topics with three to five terms per student plus an additional five terms; terms may pertain to one concept or multiple concepts. (If more than one group is to play at the same time, prepare different sets of terms for each group.)
- Cards for terms and definitions (on separate cards)
- Markers
- No score sheet is needed for this game.

Set-up:

1. Write terms on vocabulary cards.

2. Divide the cards among the students; give students blank cards where they write the definitions, using reliable sources to find the meanings. *Note the variation on page 26.*

3. Keep out three to five vocabulary cards for each student in the team. Shuffle the remaining vocabulary cards with all the definition cards.

4. Give three to five vocabulary cards to each student. Place the shuffled cards face down in the middle of the table.

Directions for THE LAST WORD:

1. Students turn their cards face up so everyone can read the science terms.

2. One student draws a card from the center pile. If it is a definition card, that student must read the card aloud and match it to a term from the students' card collections.

3. That player keeps the matched pair.

4. If the card has a vocabulary term, it is added to that player's hand.

5. If no one has the match to the definition card, or if the person who has drawn the card does not know it is a match, that person must say "No Match" and place the card on the bottom of a face-down deck of cards.

6. If it is a match to someone's card, and the player who drew the card does not know this, another player (including players who have run out of vocabulary cards) can say "Match" as soon as he or she hears "No Match." If the challenger can make the correct match, he or she keeps the matched pair.

Continued on next page.

7. If the player who drew the card or the challenger makes a wrong match, that player must give up a vocabulary card, placing it on the bottom of the center pile.

8. Continue the game, moving clockwise around the table, until all matches are made. A player can continue to participate after his or her cards are gone.

9. To keep on their toes, students must be alert for the last word. As soon as a student sees that one word is left, he or she should call out, **"The last word!"** If the correct match is made, that pair of cards gets a double score (the student can count it twice).

10. The player who has collected the most matches is the winner.

* Variation: Beyond the Definitions

Instead of writing definitions, students become comfortable enough with a term to *draw* something that communicates its meaning. Students then proceed with the game to match science terms with visual representations—taking the task to a more complex level.

After the game:

Students work together in pairs or teams of three to set science terms to rhythm. They choose one term and create a rap to share with others. The rap must present the term in a way that explains its meaning and purpose, application, or implications.

GAME #3   Pay, Pass, Play

Teams

Game Objective: Each team tries to make the most matches of terms with their definitions or descriptions.

Supplies:

- Collection of science terms (including symbols and formulas) on a topic or concept
- Teacher-prepared DEFINITION-DESCRIPTION sheet with definitions or descriptions for all or most of the terms *Note the variation on page 29.*
- Cards for terms and definitions (on separate cards)
- Markers
- Dice (one die per team)
- Play money ($1 bills and a few $5 bills totaling $25 per team)
- Extra play money for the bank (teacher)
- Copy of PAY, PASS, PLAY Score Sheet for each student (page 30)

Set-up:

1. Prepare PAY, PASS, PLAY Score Sheets for students. These will have definitions or descriptions for the terms that students will identify in this game.

2. Prepare cards with vocabulary terms written one per card. (Include a few terms/cards that are not defined on the PAY, PASS, PLAY Score Sheet.)

3. Post the cards face down on a desk or table.

4. Number the back side (side facing students) of each card in sequential order.

5. Divide students into six teams, assigning each team a number 1 to 6.

6. Give each team a die and $25.

7. Give each student a PAY, PASS, PLAY Score Sheet.

Directions for PAY, PASS, PLAY

1. Allow a few minutes for teams to look over the definitions-descriptions and attempt to identify terms that would match the definition or description. These should be written under the "Likely Match" column.

2. Begin the game with Team 1. (The next round will start with team 2 and so on.)

3. One team member chooses a number from the back of one of the cards.

4. Turn over the card to reveal the vocabulary term to the whole class.

5. Team 1 will decide if they want to **PLAY** or **PASS.**

Continued on next page.

6. If they choose to **PLAY,** the student who chose the number reads the definition or description that he or she believes matches the term. If the definition is correct, the bank pays the team $1, and the card with the term is given to that team.

7. If the team chooses to **PLAY** and the wrong definition is read, the team pays $1 to the bank. The vocabulary card is placed, face down, back on the desk or table.

8. If the team decides to **PASS,** someone in the team rolls the die. The team with the number rolled on the die receives the **PASS** and **must** attempt to identify the matching definition.

9. If the team receiving the **PASS** answers correctly, the team who passed must pay them $2. If the team who receives the **PASS** answers incorrectly, they must pay $2 to the team from whom they received the **PASS.** If answered incorrectly, the vocabulary card returns to its face-down position on the desk or table.

10. If a team selects a card that does not have a matching definition and is able to give a correct definition or description, the bank pays that team a $3 bonus. In addition, that team will still receive the usual $1 from the bank or the $2 payout if the card came to them with a **PASS.** If they give an incorrect definition, they pay the bank $1.

11. As matches are made, individual students keep records of the actual match results on their score sheets

12. When all matches have been completed on the definition sheet, continue the rounds with the extra vocabulary words. These terms may also be used to break a tie.

13. At the end of the game, each team tallies the number of correctly matched terms and the amount of money. The money is divided as evenly as possible among team members. (Decide how to allocate the uneven amounts; this might be given to students who contributed the most.) Each student records this information on individual score sheets.

14. By the end of the game, all students should have completed their PAY, PASS, PLAY Score Sheets. Those who do not must pay the bank $1 for each missing definition or description.

15. The team with the highest total for correct matches plus individual money wins the game.

16. Final points and individual money earned may be used toward determining student scores or grades for the activity.

17. To further enhance students' engagement, let students use the play money to purchase extra credit points, or small rewards such as food or gadgets.

Continued on next page.

*Variation: Beyond the Definitions

Instead of giving definitions or descriptions to students, prepare a handout that lists several **brief scenarios or situations.** You might change the title on the handout to WHAT'S GOING ON? As vocabulary cards are turned over and a team decides to PLAY, they will have to decide what scenario matches the term. Of course, they will need to understand the meaning in order to make this judgment.

Sample scenarios:

The magician thought no one could see the trick behind his curtain. Alas! The fabric was so thin that the entire ruse was revealed to the audience! *(transparent)*

"I could push this motorcycle home, but it would be a lot easier if I had some gasoline!" complained Ted. *(chemical energy)*

Leo was capable of raking the yard. He just had to convince himself to get off the couch first. *(potential energy)*

The force of the pool cue sent the white ball smashing into the static orange ball. The white ball stopped, and the orange ball headed into the pocket. *(Law of Conservation of Energy)*

After the game:

Ask students to identify the terms that they understand least. Each student chooses one such term and finds out more about it in a given amount of time. Then, the student becomes a campaign manager for that term. The task is to treat that term like a candidate in an election. The word or phrase could be running for the office of most powerful, practical, prestigious, versatile, or influential science term. Each student creates a campaign poster, platform, or speech for the "candidate." (The class can actually hold an "election," voting for words based on the presentations by the campaign managers.)

PAY, PASS, PLAY Score Sheet

Student Name _____

Likely Match	Definition or Description	Actual Match

Team #	# Correct Team Matches	Total Team $ Amount	Individual $ Amount	# Items NOT Completed	Amount $ Owed to Bank from	Total Correct Matches & Individual $

Definition or Description	Actual Match
Electricity flows in one path	*series circuit*
Relationship among current, voltage, and resistance	*Ohm's Law*
The lowest point of a wave	*trough*
Point on a longitudinal wave that is spread apart	*rarefraction*
ROYGBIV	*visible light*
Material through which light is transmitted	*transparent*
Ability to do work	*energy*
The unit for frequency	*hertz*
Travels through space	*electromagnetic waves*
Stored energy	*potential energy*
The bouncing back of light rays	*reflection*
Energy cannot be created or destroyed	*Law of Conservation of Energy*
Incoming light rays that strike a surface	*incident ray*
Allows electricity and/or heat to flow through easily	*conductor*
The highness and lowness of sound	*pitch*
Light waves with the lowest frequency	*radio waves*
Food, gasoline, and batteries are examples	*chemical energy*
Force that moves an object a distance	*work*
Energy of motion	*kinetic energy*
Material that does not transmit light	*opaque*
Wave that moves up and down	*transverse*
The bending of light waves	*refraction*
Electricity flows in more than one path	*parallel circuit*
Requires a medium to travel through	*mechanical waves*
Light waves with the shortest wavelength	*gamma*
Material through which electricity/heat does not flow through easily	*insulator*
Break in the circuit	*open circuit*
The number of waves that pass a point per second	*frequency*
Sound is an example of this type of wave	*longitudinal*
Relates to the energy of a wave	*amplitude*
Material that transmits some light; image is fuzzy	*translucent*
The highest point of a wave	*crest*

Team #	# Correct Team Matches	Total Team $ Amount	Individual $ Amount	# Items NOT Completed	Amount $ Owed to Bank from	Total Correct Matches & Individual $

GAME #4 *Stop the Game!* Teams

Game Objective: Students hear repetitions of terms and meanings as teams compete to be the first in each round to match all cards.

Supplies:

- Collection of science terms (including symbols and formulas) pertaining to one topic or concept, such as *force and motion* (Have enough terms to assign one to each student. Each team will be given different sets of terms.)
- Cards for terms and definitions (on separate cards)
- Markers
- STOP THE GAME! Score Sheet for each team (page 34)

Set-up:

1. Divide students into teams.

2. Give a list of vocabulary terms to each team, with one word per student. Supply enough cards for terms and definition.

3. Give a few STOP THE GAME! Score Sheets to each team.

4. Each student takes one word and prepares a card with that term and a second card with the definition. ***Note the variation on page 33.***

Directions for STOP THE GAME!

1. Within each team, students shuffle the word cards and definition cards together and spread them out, face down, on the table.

2. At the GO signal, students turn over the cards and match definitions with terms.

3. When a team completes all matches, the team members stand and say "Stop the Game!" When the first team stands, all other teams must stop matching and listen. Students on the standing team share their matches by reading them aloud.

4. All other teams, in turn, will share the matches they had at the moment the game was stopped.

5. Points for the round are based on the number of correct matches. Teams award themselves one point for every correct match. They deduct one point for each incorrect match from the total number of correct matches.

6. At the end of the round, after scores are recorded on the score sheet, teams shuffle the cards together and pass them face down to the team on their right.

7. The game begins again and follows the same process as in steps 2-6 above.

Continued on next page.

8. The game continues until all sets of cards are successfully matched.

9. The team with the most points wins the game.

Alternate game: Put a time limit on each round to see how many matches can be made in the allotted time. This makes the game more challenging.

*Variation: Beyond the Definitions

Instead of finding and writing definitions, students consider the **_setting_** in which the term might be found. Each student uses the second card to write a location where the item, unit, process, or descriptor might be found (e.g., for *oxidation,* the student might write *in a damp garage;* for *alkaline,* the student might write *a swimming pool;* and for *regular intervals,* the student might write *a heartbeat).*

After the game:

Randomly assign five of the terms to each student. Students enter the terms on a chart like this and complete the chart. This will give an assessment of how well the student understands the terms. Students can gather in pairs or small groups to share the information on these reflection charts. For students who have any checkmarks in the final column, group members can take on the challenge of helping them understand the words better.

Term	I know the meaning (Here it is.)	I can give an example. (Here it is.)	I know another term related to this. (Here it is.)	I need more experience with this word. (Check if true.)

GAME #4

STOP THE GAME! SCORE SHEET

Team Members:

Rounds	Vocabulary Words Matched	Number of Points Earned

Rounds	Vocabulary Words Matched	Number of Points Earned

Rounds	Vocabulary Words Matched	Number of Points Earned

Rounds	Vocabulary Words Matched	Number of Points Earned
Total Points _____		

GAME #5   *Science Slap*   **Individual Small Group**

Game Objective: Collect the most matches of terms and their meanings by the end of the game.

Supplies:

- Collection of science terms (including symbols and formulas) on one topic or multiple topics with several terms per student (If more than one team is to play at the same time, prepare different sets of terms for each team.)
- Cards for terms and definitions (on separate cards)
- Markers
- No score sheet is needed for this game.

Set-up:

1. Give the list of vocabulary terms to the team. If you use the variation suggested below, choose terms that students will be able to demonstrate.

2. Students write the terms on cards and the definitions on separate cards.

3. Shuffle the vocabulary cards and definition cards separately.

Directions for SCIENCE SLAP:

1. Distribute vocabulary cards evenly to players.

2. Players do not look at the cards but place them face down on the table.

3. Place the deck of definition cards face down in the center of the table.

4. One player begins the game by turning over a definition card and reading it aloud. ***Note the variation on page 36.***

5. Then each player, one at a time, moving clockwise around the table, turns over the top card on his or her stack and tosses it in the center of the table. This continues until the vocabulary card matching the definition card that was read aloud is played.

Continued on next page.

6. When the matching vocabulary card is tossed out, the first player to slap that card gets the definition card and ALL the vocabulary cards tossed out to that point—IF the SLAP was correct. The vocabulary card AND the matching definition card are then removed from the pile and kept aside by the player who made the correct match.

7. If the player who did the SLAP was incorrect, the game continues until the correct card is played. (Optional: a rule might be made that bans this player from contributing cards during the next round of play.)

8. The teachers or others on the team must verify a correct or incorrect SLAP.

9. The game ends when all definition cards have been matched. The player with the most matches wins.

*Variation: Beyond the Definitions

When a player draws a definition card from the deck, he or she reads it silently and does not share it with other students. Instead, the player ***demonstrates the term or a concept*** or process related to it. The player may narrate the demonstration, but must be careful NOT to name the term in any form.

After the game:

Students work in pairs or teams to create a puzzle with some of the terms. They may use puzzle templates from the Internet or work with interactive apps, craft 3-D puzzles, or put puzzles on paper. In order to work the puzzle, other students must understand or research the terms.

GAME #6 *Where's the Match?* **Teams**

Game Objective: Match as many terms as possible with correct definitions.

Supplies:

- Collection of science terms (including symbols and formulas) on one topic (one term per student)
- Cards for terms and definitions (on separate cards)
- Markers
- WHERE'S THE MATCH? Score Sheets for all students (page 39)
- Tape or other substance for posting cards

Set-up:

1. Assign a vocabulary term to each student.

2. Students write the terms on cards and the term meanings on separate cards. ***Note the variation on page 38.***

3. Collect all the cards. Shuffle the vocabulary cards and definition cards separately.

4. Divide students into teams. Pass out vocabulary and definition cards randomly. See that each team has some of each kind of card, but the amounts do not have to be equal. If any cards are left over, keep those cards and post them on a display wall so students will be able to see them during the game.

5. Give each student a WHERE'S THE MATCH? Score Sheet.

Directions for WHERE'S THE MATCH?

1. Students on each team match as many terms and definitions as they can from their cards and set them aside. They spread the remaining cards face down on their table.

2. The first team describes their matches aloud to the rest of the class. Each correct match is worth one point.

3. Continue with this until all teams have described their initial matches.

4. Beginning again with the first team, each student turns over a card and reads it aloud, giving the matching term or definition from his or her background knowledge.

5. If the term or definition is correct, that person checks the display board to see if the matching card is there. That card is given to the team and the team earns one point.

Continued on next page.

6. If the matching card is not on the display board, the student makes a guess as to which other team has the matching card. If the term or definition and the guess are both correct, the team in possession of the card gives it up. The receiving team earns one point. If the guess is incorrect, the unmatched card is turned face down again.

7. If the correct team is selected to have the matching card, that team must give it up to the team that made the match.

8. When a team earns a point from guessing the correct team, the person who made the guess can take a card from any other team in the room without looking at what is on the card. If the card taken happens to match a card in possession of that same team, the receiving team earns another point by reading the cards aloud.

9. This process continues until all terms and definitions have been matched. When a team runs out of cards, they are out of the game and other teams continue without them.

10. As the game continues, team members use their score sheets to keep records of the matches.

11. At the end of the game, the team with the most points is the winner.

*Variation: Beyond the Definitions

Instead of writing definitions on the second set of cards, students create and **write a question** about the term (without naming the term). Ask them to think of questions that get at complete meanings of the terms; i.e., to answer the question, another student will need to understand the related concept.

After the game:

Students work alone or in pairs to turn terms into showstoppers! They plan a way to visually promote the word, phrase, formula, or symbol and the concept it addresses. One possibility is to use digital cameras to make short videos. When they are satisfied with the videos, they can text or email them or post them on the class website.

WHERE'S THE MATCH? SCORE SHEET

Team Members:

Vocabulary Term	Definition
Total # of Correct Matches	

GAME #7 *Master the Matrix* **Teams**

Game Objective: Get the most matches of terms and their meanings; assign terms to reasonable categories.

Supplies:

- Collection of science terms (including symbols and formulas) in four to six different categories (five or more terms per category)
  Use terms from various areas of science (e.g., Life, Earth, Space, and Physical Science) or various content within one topic (e.g., force and motion, energy, work, electricity).
- Large cards for terms and card strips for definitions
- Markers
- MASTER THE MATRIX Score Sheets for all students (page 42)
- Tape or other substance for posting cards

Set-up:

1. Write vocabulary terms on cards and matching definitions on strips.

2. Write headings on the board that correlate with the different content. (For example, write *states of matter, chemical reactions, physical properties,* etc.) These headings will form the titles of columns for a matrix.

3. Finish creating the matrix by writing point values in the rows below the headings. For example, the first row might have a value of 5 points all the way across the columns, the second might be 10 points, then 20 points, and so on.

4. Tape the vocabulary cards face down on the board in the point-value sections under the correct headings. Place the terms in order from easiest to most difficult. Place the cards so that the point values show in each row, or write point values on backs of the cards.

5. Divide students into teams. Pass out definition strips randomly, giving the same number to each student.

6. Give a MASTER THE MATRIX Score Sheet to each student.

Directions for MASTER THE MATRIX:

1. Students review all the definitions given to their team. Then they spread the definition strips in the center of their table.

Continued on next page.

2. Beginning with one team, a member chooses a category and an amount that he or she thinks may match one of the team's definitions.

3. That student turns the vocabulary card face up on the board and reads the vocabulary card aloud. A member of the team holding the correct definition must stand and read the definition. ***Note the variation below.***

4. If the definition is a correct match, that vocabulary card and the corresponding points go to the team that gave the definition. The game continues to another round with the next team choosing a category.

5. If an incorrect definition is read by the team that chose the category, or if no one stands from the team that chose the category, a member from another team may stand and give the definition in his or her own words. It the definition is correct, that team gets the vocabulary card, the definition strip, and the points.

6. If an incorrect definition is read or stated by another team, the number of points for that vocabulary term is subtracted from that team's score. An unmatched card is turned face down on the board for another round. Make a note of any terms that any students have difficulty matching.

7. Continue rounds until all terms have been correctly matched to definitions. As the game play goes along, students should record the team's points on the MASTER THE MATRIX Score Sheet.

8. The team with the most points wins the game.

*Variation: Beyond the Definitions

In step 3 of the game, instead of reading the definition of the term aloud, a team member **uses body movements** (no words) to show a result of the term or concept (something that happens because of its existence or use).

After the game:

Make a list of terms that posed difficulty for any students during the game. Pairs of students draw a term from this list at random and create a cartoon or collage that teaches the meaning of the term.

MASTER THE MATRIX Score Sheet

Team members _____ **Topic** _____

Vocabulary Word Correctly Matched	# of Points Received or Subtracted from Match (indicate with + or - signs in front of the amounts)
Total Points:	

GAME #8   *Vocabulary Scavenger Hunt*   **Teams**

Game Objective: Find the most hidden terms and match them with the correct description or meaning.

Note: This game uses concepts in the field of Space Science, but the process can be applied to any science topic.

Supplies:

- Collection of science terms (including symbols and formulas) on a broad topic that students have studied or will study
- Cards for vocabulary terms
- Markers
- VOCABULARY SCAVENGER HUNT Term List with Definitions for the teacher (pages 46 and 47) ***Note the variation on page 45.***
- Copies of VOCABULARY SCAVENGER HUNT Student Log for all students (pages 49 and 49)
- Tape or other substance for securing strips
- No score sheet is needed for this game.

Set-up:

1. Make vocabulary cards on strips of colored paper or cardstock. Write, type, or copy each of the science terms on small strips of colored paper. (Keep to one color.) If possible, laminate them to preserve them for future use. Since the strips will be hidden, the use of colored paper (rather than white) will make them easier to find.

2. Before students arrive in class, hide the strips with vocabulary terms around the room. Use tape to secure strips under desks or other locations where they need to be suspended. If other students help with the hiding, specify locations where they should not be hidden. For example, it's time consuming for students to search inside books or drawers. The strips should not be folded, rolled, or altered in any manner. Look for clever and surprising locations—such as on the bottom of the teacher's shoe, inside the wastebasket, or tucked into a rolled-up map. If this game is played with subsequent classes, you may choose to have students who complete the game hide the strips for the next class.

3. Number the board or a wall in sequential order to match the numbers of definitions on the definition list. Leave enough space next to each number for students to tape the strips beside the matching definition numbers.

Continued on next page.

4. Group students in small teams. Assign each team a letter (e.g., Team A, Team B…). The number of teams depends on the number of students you want on the floor during the search, as there will be one student from each team searching at any one time.

5. Give a VOCABULARY SCAVENGER HUNT Student Log sheet to each student.

Directions for VOCABULARY SCAVENGER HUNT:

1. If this game is used as a unit review, allow teams a few minutes to review the definitions-descriptions list. If this game is used to introduce or preview the unit, allow students the use of resources throughout the search or let them complete the list a day ahead of the search.

2. Tell students that they'll be doing a scavenger hunt for science terms related to the unit of study. Let them know about the strips hidden around the room and about specific locations where they are NOT hidden.

3. Emphasize that **only one** team member is allowed to search at any given time, and that all students must take turns participating in the search. Each team must try to give each student an equal number of turns searching.

4. During a person's search, he or she may find **one strip.**

5. Once a strip is found, that person must sit back down with his or her team to find the matching definition or description. As soon as a team member sits to find his or her match, another member may get up to search, so long as that member's previous match has been posted and verified to be correct.

6. When a student thinks he or she has found the correct match, the strip should be posted to the board or wall beside the number that corresponds with the definitions or descriptions on the student log. The student must also write his or her team's assigned letter beside the word taped to the board or wall.

7. The teacher continuously watches to verify the matches taped to the board or wall. If a term is correctly placed, the teacher marks it with a large check so all students can record this on their lists. If a term is placed incorrectly, the teacher quickly identifies the team and asks the team member to retrieve the strip. The team member continues to look for the correct match of a definition or description.

8. If team members fail to follow the rules, his or her entire team can be banned from searching for a period of time.

9. Once all the matches are found and posted correctly or the time runs out, the game ends.

Continued on next page.

10. The teacher tallies the number of matches for each team, based on the letters written on the board or wall.

11. The team with the most matches wins the game.

*Variation: Beyond the Definitions

Instead of preparing a list of definitions or descriptions, ask this question about each term:

> *What difference does it make?* Write a headline for a news flash about the chosen term to **communicate what influence, benefit, or effect** that term (and the concept to which it is connected) has in the real world. Do not include the term in the headline. Students match these, instead of definitions, to the terms.

After the game:

Students work in pairs to identify a term that intrigues them most. They outline a short WebQuest that other students can follow to learn more about the complexity and application of the term. Or, if the suggested game variation has been used, students can choose one of the headlines and write or orally share the news flash that would be written to elaborate on what difference that term makes.

VOCABULARY SCAVENGER HUNT
Term List with Definitions-Descriptions

1. meteoroids	A chunk of rock that moves through Earth's solar system; it does not enter Earth's atmosphere.	
2. meteor	A chunk of rock that burns up in Earth's atmosphere	
3. meteorite	A chunk of rock that strikes Earth's surface	
4. comet	A mass of rock, dust, and ice that has a burning tail that points away from the sun	
5. asteroid	Small, rocky bodies that are mostly found between Mars and Jupiter	
6. terrestrial	Planets composed of rock and dirt; the inner planets	
7. one	The number of stars in Earth's solar system	
8. billions	The number of stars in Earth's galaxy	
9. tides	These are caused mainly by the moon's gravitational pull	
10. 29.5	The number of days it takes the moon to complete one orbit around Earth	
11. moon phases	These occur because the moon orbits around Earth and different portions of the sunlit side of the moon are visible from Earth.	
12. solar eclipse	This occurs when the moon casts a shadow on a portion of Earth's surface because the moon is between the sun and Earth.	
13. lunar eclipse	This occurs when Earth casts a shadow on the moon because Earth is between the sun and the moon.	
14. seasons	These occur because Earth is tilted on its axis as it revolves around the sun.	
15. rotates on its axis	Because Earth does this, our sun seems to move across the sky.	
16. inertia	Gravity and this factor are the reasons the planets stay in orbit around the sun.	
17. distance between	Mass and this factor are what determine the amount of gravitational pull objects objects exert on each other.	
18. the inner planets	These planets are composed of a crust, a mantle, and a core.	
19. the outer planets	These planets are composed primarily of gases.	
20. Pluto	Because of its size, this planet is no longer classified as a planet.	
21. Neptune	This planet is the eighth planet in Earth's solar system.	
22. Venus	Because of its dense CO_2 atmosphere, this planet is known as "the greenhouse in the sky."	
23. Saturn	With the lowest density of all the planets in Earth's solar system, this planet could float on water.	

Continued on next page.

24. Mars	This planet has the largest volcano of all the planets in Earth's solar system.
25. Mercury	This planet takes 88 days to make one revolution around the sun.
26. Earth	This planet takes 365.25 days to make one revolution around the sun.
27. Uranus	This planet is tilted on its side; its rings extend north and south.
28. Jupiter	This planet has a giant red spot caused by a huge storm.
29. 4.6 billion years	This is the estimated age of Earth's solar system.
30. nebular theory	This is the theory of the formation of Earth's solar system.
31. blue	This is the color of the hottest stars in the sky.
32. red	This is the color of the coolest stars in the sky.
33. main sequence	90% of all stars visible from Earth are this type.
34. the sun	The star around which Earth and other planets in its solar system revolve
35. medium	This is the size of Earth's star. It is a main sequence star like 90% of the stars.
36. white dwarf	When Earth's star burns out, it will turn into a red giant, then become this type of star.
37. black hole	A super giant star will either become a neutron star or this when it dies out.
38. supernova	This is a huge explosion that occurs at the end of a super giant's life cycle.
39. nuclear fusion	Stars shine because of this.
40. light year	This is the distance light travels in a year.
41. neutron star	When a super giant dies out, it will either turn into this or a black hole.
42. Milky Way	This is the name of Earth's galaxy.
43. spiral	This is the shape of Earth's galaxy.
44. 10-20 billion years	This is the estimated age of the universe.
45. The Big Bang	This is one theory of the formation of the universe.
46. super giants	These stars burn out the fastest because they use up their energy most quickly due to their mass.
47. helium	When nuclear fusion occurs, hydrogen atoms fuse to form these atoms.
48. winter	This is the season experienced in the northern hemisphere when it is tilted away from the sun.
49. gases	The outer planets are made of this matter.
50. nebula	This is known as the birthplace of a star.

VOCABULARY SCAVENGER HUNT
Student log

Student Name _____

1. _____ A chunk of rock that moves through Earth's solar system; it does not enter Earth's atmosphere.

2. _____ A chunk of rock that burns up in Earth's atmosphere

3. _____ A chunk of rock that strikes Earth's surface

4. _____ A mass of rock, dust, and ice that has a burning tail that points away from the sun

5. _____ Small, rocky bodies that are mostly found between Mars and Jupiter

6. _____ Planets composed of rock and dirt; the inner planets

7. _____ The number of stars in Earth's solar system

8. _____ The number of stars in Earth's galaxy

9. _____ These are caused mainly by the moon's gravitational pull

10. _____ The number of days it takes the moon to complete one orbit around Earth

11. _____ These occur because the moon orbits around Earth and different portions of the sunlit half of the moon are visible from Earth.

12. _____ This occurs when the moon casts a shadow on a portion of Earth's surface because the moon is between the sun and Earth.

13. _____ This occurs when Earth casts a shadow on the moon because Earth is between the sun and the moon.

14. _____ These occurs because Earth is tilted on its axis as it revolves around the sun.

15. _____ Because Earth does this, our sun seems to move across the sky.

16. _____ Gravity and this factor are the reasons the planets stay in orbit around the sun.

17. _____ Mass and this factor are what determine the amount of gravitational pull objects exert on each other.

18. _____ These planets are composed of a crust, a mantle, and a core.

19. _____ These planets are composed of primarily gases.

20. _____ Because of its size, this planet is no longer classified as a planet.

21. _____ This planet is the eighth planet in Earth's solar system.

22. _____ Because of its dense CO_2 atmosphere, this planet is known as "the greenhouse in the sky."

Continued on next page.

23. _____ With the lowest density of all the planets in Earth's solar system, this planet could float on water.

24. _____ This planet has the largest volcano of all the planets in Earth's solar system.

25. _____ This planet takes 88 days to make one revolution around the sun.

26. _____ This planet takes 365.25 days to make one revolution around the sun.

27. _____ This planet is tilted on its side; its rings extend north and south.

28. _____ This planet has a giant red spot caused by a huge storm.

29. _____ This is the estimated age of Earth's solar system.

30. _____ This is the theory of the formation of Earth's solar system.

31. _____ This is the color of the hottest stars in the sky.

32. _____ This is the color of the coolest stars in the sky.

33. _____ 90% of all stars visible from Earth are this type.

34. _____ The star around which Earth and other planets in its solar system revolve

35. _____ This is the size of Earth's star. It is a main sequence star like 90% of the stars.

36. _____ When Earth's star burns out, it will turn into a red giant, then become this type of star.

37. _____ A super giant star will either become a neutron star or this when it dies out.

38. _____ This is a huge explosion that occurs at the end of a super giant's life cycle.

39. _____ Stars shine because of this.

40. _____ This is the distance light travels in a year.

41. _____ When a super giant dies out, it will either turn into this or a black hole.

42. _____ This is the name of Earth's galaxy.

43. _____ This is the shape of Earth's galaxy.

44. _____ This is the estimated age of the universe.

45. _____ This is one theory of the formation of the universe.

46. _____ These stars burn out the fastest because they use up their energy most quickly due to their mass.

47. _____ When nuclear fusion occurs, hydrogen atoms fuse to form these atoms.

48. _____ This is the season experienced in the northern hemisphere when it is tilted away from the sun.

49. _____ The outer planets are made of this matter.

50. _____ This is known as the birthplace of a star.

GAME #9 *Answers for Sale*   Teams

Game Objective: Every student answers every question satisfactorily; the team spends as little money as possible to gain answers.

Supplies:

- Collection of science terms (including symbols and formulas) that relate to concepts on a topic that students have studied or will study
- Collection of questions, one related to each of the terms
- Copies of ANSWERS FOR SALE Question Sheet for all students
- Question-Assignment Chart (See sample below.)
- Rotation Plan for game (See sample below.)
- Resources for students to investigate questions
- Play money (mostly $1 bills)
- Dice or spinners for each team
- No score sheet is needed for this game.

Set-up:

1. Prepare questions that include the use of science terms. The questions should take some research, thinking, and understanding of the concepts included. Title this sheet ANSWERS FOR SALE Question Sheet. Leave room for students to answer the questions.

2. Prepare a chart that shows the class which questions are assigned to which groups. As you distribute questions among teams, give each team an equal number of easy or complex questions.

Team 1	Team 2	Team 3	Team 4	Team 5
1	2	3	4	5
6	7	8	9	10
11	12	13	14	15
16	17	18	19	20
21	22	23	24	25

3. Assign students to teams. Give a copy of the ANSWERS FOR SALE Question Sheet to each student. Students write their team number on the sheet. At the end of the game, each student is expected to have answered every question.

Continued on next page.

4. Give each team adequate reference and other suitable materials to answer questions, $50 in play money, and a die or spinner. (The dice or spinners will be used for teams to find how much they'll pay to buy answers to questions. Students could design their own spinners with amounts of $1, $2, $3, and $4.)

5. Teams get ready for the game by finding the answers to their assigned questions. Allow about 20 minutes for this, and then verify answers that are correct. If all the questions are not answered, students may continue this answering process after the game begins.

Directions for ANSWERS FOR SALE:

1. The teacher explains the rules for rotations (2-9 below) and posts a rotation chart to show the system for buying answers from other teams. This chart shows an example:

Round 1 (5-6 minutes)	Round 2 (3-4 minutes)	Round 3 (3-4 minutes)	Round 4 (3-4 minutes)	Round 5 (5-6 minutes)
Group 1 to Group 2	Group 1 to Group 3	Group 1 to Group 4	Group 1 to Group 5	During this round, the group member will go to any other groups to buy as many answers as possible during the allotted time.
G 2 to G 3	G 2 to G 4	G 2 to G 5	G 2 to G 1	
G 3 to G 4	G 3 to G 5	G 3 to G 1	G 3 to G 2	
G 4 to G 5	G 4 to G 1	G 4 to G 2	G 4 to G 3	
G 5 to G 1	G 5 to G 2	G 5 to G 3	G 5 to G 4	

2. Before a round begins, a team decides the maximum amount of money that will be spent buying answers from another team during that round. The team also identifies which answer(s) they wish to buy.

3. When a round begins, one person from a team rotates to the group identified on the rotation chart. The player takes along a copy of the questions and some money. That player rolls a die or spins the spinner to see how much an answer will cost. If the player has enough money to do so, he or she may buy more than one answer from that team.

4. While one player is rotating, the other players on the team continue to find answers to questions. By answering questions on its own, the team will save money during the game. However, each team MUST buy at least one answer from each of the other groups.

Continued on next page.

5. When the roving player returns to his or her team, all students must copy the answer(s) bought from the other team.

6. The game continues with other rounds. Each student on a team must get a rotation turn (if there are enough rounds).

7. During Round 5, the roving player may go to any of the other teams and buy as many answers as possible during the allotted time (or the money runs out). During this final round, teams may bargain by offering deals on the answers (i.e., "two answers for the price of one").

8. The individual teams must find any answer that is not purchased from another team. Allow some time for students to finish writing all answers, counting money, and reporting remaining money to the teacher

9. The team with the most money remaining wins the game, provided that team has all answers verified to be correct. You might arrange for money to be used to buy extra credit points or snacks or other small prizes.

10. Completed question sheets can serve as notes or study-guides for further review of the topic.

After the game:

In this game, teams have worked hard to find and understand answers to questions about a science topic. They can pass that hard work on to teach others what they've learned. Provide time for teams to choose the key questions they believe will best help to teach some of the concepts. Working together, team members write and polish the information that they'd like to teach in a question-answer format. They may augment the questions with diagrams, drawings, photos, or other graphics. The team then decides where they will post the information. Depending on school policies, it might be on a posting site (such as Pinterest), a class website or wiki, an email, social network page, SMS, or blog. After securing a free QR code app (www.qustuff.com; qrcode.kaywa.com), the team generates a QR code that will link other students to the digital destination where they've parked the teaching tool.

GAME #10 *Student Performance Task* *Design-a-Game*

Teams

Game Objective: Students develop card games or board games to introduce, teach, review, or strengthen understanding of concepts in a particular science topic or unit.

Suggested supplies:

- dice
- spinners
- play money
- poster board
- index cards
- buttons, clothespins, or other small items used for game pieces
- sports equipment
- technological devices
- any other items needed as determined by the game design
- copies of DESIGN-A-GAME Planning Sheet for all teams (page 55)
- copies of DESIGN-A-GAME Reflection Sheets for all teams (page 56)

Set-up:

1. Gather the class together to reflect on other vocabulary games they have played. Think about and discuss other kinds of games that could be used to learn or review vocabulary terms. Enjoy brainstorming and comparing ideas.

2. At the end of a science unit, divide students into small teams. Give a copy of the DESIGN-A-GAME Planning Sheet to each team.

Directions for DESIGN-A-GAME:

1. Explain that the task for each team is to create a vocabulary game using terms from the just-completed unit. The game must help students review, expand, and communicate understanding of science terms and the concepts they represent.

2. Tell students that they are not limited to card games or board games. They might design carnival games, versions of TV game shows, or games based on competitive sports.

Continued on next page.

3. Students may begin by forming a list of vocabulary terms, concepts, or processes from the unit of study.

4. Give students plenty of planning time to imagine and design a game. Teams will also need time to create the game materials, write the instructions, and test the game. The DESIGN-A-GAME Planning Sheets will help them think through their ideas.

5. Once the games are completed and tested, schedule time and ways for students to play each others' games. Invite another class to play the games too!

After the task:

• Take advantage of the wonderful opportunities for formative assessment during and after this task. As students design and play games, you'll have many chances to observe how well students understand the concepts and terminology.

• In addition to using the game-design approach as a review or culminating activity, students may design games to teach the concepts to other students. This expands the instructional and assessment opportunities!

• Use the DESIGN-A-GAME Reflection Sheet as a way to evaluate student performance on the task. This form combines self-reflection (by the team), peer-reflection (by another team), and teacher reflection on the game-design task.

GAME #10

PERFORMANCE TASK
DESIGN-A-GAME Planning Sheet

Team Members_____

_____

Science unit topic:

Terms or concepts to be reviewed:

Name of the game:

Object of the game:

Materials needed (things we'll use or make):

How we will set up the game:

How to play the game:

How to score the game:

GAME #10

PERFORMANCE TASK
DESIGN-A-GAME Reflection Sheet

Name of the Game _____ **Science Topic** _____

Team Members _____

Give a 1 to 3 rating for each category:

1 = Excellent   2 = Strong   3 = Needs Improvement

Performance Categories	Self Review *Name*	Peer Review *Name*	Teacher Review *Name*
The game covers a minimum of 15 terms or concepts, used correctly.			
The game is creative and engaging. Others seem to enjoy playing it.			
The game is creative or original. It is a new idea or clever adaptation of an existing game.			
The game is neatly designed and the components are well organized.			
The game includes well-defined, clear instructions for how to play.			
The game is easy to follow and play without confusion.			
This game really works to help students strengthen understanding of the science terminology or concepts.			
All members of the team participated in creation of the game and worked well together.			

Strengths of this game:

Chapter 2
Science Literacy Stations

Learning stations are a perfect fit for upper intermediate and secondary classrooms (grades 6 through 12)! Since students in this age group have already developed many reading, writing, and thinking skills that allow a good measure of self-direction, stations offer great possibilities for independent or small-group activities. Numerous concepts, skills, and processes can be introduced, taught, reviewed, or assessed at a learning station. This chapter presents a sampling of learning station options that can be used to teach, extend, or assess science literacy.

Setting the Overall Plan

A classroom may have a few or many stations. This will depend on your goals, space, available resources, and class format. The ideas in this chapter are based on a model in which the whole class, broken into small groups, uses stations simultaneously. The stations all focus on a broad science topic or unit, but each station approaches the topic differently or works on different, related concepts. It's ideal to have several stations through which all students can rotate over one or more class periods. Plan activities that can be done by a group of three to five students.

Setting the Purpose

Decide what each station will offer or accomplish. Is the goal to ignite interest in a new science topic? To review and strengthen concepts already taught? To follow up on lessons to assess and deepen understandings? To experiment and discover? To analyze and evaluate information expressed visually? To compare different scientific presentations? To look for key ideas and details in a text, or trace the development of a concept? To create a product to show their understanding of a concept? To engage in debates about a science-related issue? To ask questions or define problems? To plan an investigation? Your goals for students will determine the experiences you choose to include in the stations.

Choosing the Activities

Design activities that focus on a few specific concepts or goals. Think of one or two activities that will take no longer than 15 or 20 minutes combined to complete. As much as possible, you want all stations to take about the same amount of time so that students waiting to visit other stations will not have a lot of waiting time. As you set up each station, give it a number and a name so students can follow stations chronologically and remember where they have been! If all stations have activities pertaining to the same general topic, students will receive five or six "doses" of instruction, review, or assessment on that topic (depending on number of stations).

Keeping Things Exciting

Create stations that students will want to try! Each one should hook students from they moment they arrive. Students should leave each station invigorated at having encountered something satisfying and having elevated some skill or understanding.

- See that each station is inviting visually.

- Include succinct but sufficiently detailed instructions about what to do.

- Post information that clearly communicates to students the expected outcomes.

- Add a strong dash of surprise, cleverness, or fun.

- Include stations that ignite imagination and creativity.

- Vary the approaches, tools, and outcomes. Be sure to include technological devices, apps, programs, presentations, and short projects as part of the options in some of the stations.

- Plan for the student to leave the station with a way to show something he or she knows or can do.

- Include stations that keep students active and engaged to help them stay on task.

Using the Stations

Assign students to small groups of three to five students each. Set a schedule whereby groups rotate among stations. For example, assign Group 1 to station 1 and Groups 2 through 6 to corresponding stations. When the allotted time is elapsed, Group 1 rotates to station 2, and so on. This continues over a period of days until all groups have worked at all stations in consecutive order.

Showing Outcomes and Accountability

Give students a way to record, show, or explain what happened while at the station, or a way to respond to something in the station. The sample stations described in this chapter include a form, record-keeping sheet, or handout for each station. Use different colors for sheets at different stations to assist with organization. Make sure the station number is printed clearly on each sheet.

Differentiating Learning at the Stations

Even in a class of one grade level or one ability level, all kinds of learners will come to the science stations. Consider these different learners when you design the stations. Strive to offer options that will embrace varied styles, gifts, speeds, comfort levels, and needs. Here are a few suggestions for differentiating learning at stations:

- To level the field for students who struggle with reading, offer auditory and visual instructions along with written instructions at the station.

- When planning a set of stations around one topic, intentionally vary the approach, presentation, or products among the stations as a way to give different kinds of learners a boost at the stations that match their greatest gifts. For example, of six stations, one might be based on a video, another may include music or rhythm, another can focus on math experiences, another could require movement or demonstration, another might focus on discovery, and the last could be a listening and writing activity.

- Pair a struggling reader or writer with a partner who can transcribe the ideas for the duo.

- Find a way to give extra time for some students to finish tasks.

- Distinguish between required tasks and optional tasks at the station so that a student who needs more time can still meet the basic goal of the station.

- Allow for that student who thinks beyond (or outside of) the group to show something of an individual accomplishment—instead of or in addition to the group effort.

- Provide alternative ways for students to become involved with the science concepts presented or to show what they've learned. Students can draw, create, or speak as alternatives or supplements to written products.

- Use volunteer adults or older students from other classes to assist students in reading, writing, researching, following instructions, or in creating a finished product.

- Turn the station around! Ask students to create or add to activities or items in the station. They can ask the questions, describe the concepts, make a game, set up an experiment, or decide how to express and share outcomes. This paves the way for many different kinds of contributions from many different learners. And here's a bonus: this always deepens students' understandings of the science processes and concepts.

Extending the Learning

An "After the Station" section follows each station description. These sections suggest some options for students to expand and deepen the concepts they've learned and to apply other curriculum standards. Since the station activities are time limited, student engagement is still high when it's time to rotate to the next station. They'll love having more time later to take what they've learned and investigate, share, or explain further.

Connecting to Technology

- Integrate technology use into station activities as often as possible. Make use of programs and devices available in your school and classroom. In a particular set of stations, students should encounter technology in at least one or two of the stations.

- Some sort of a written form, evaluation, or reporting template accompanies each station in this chapter. This paper offers a way to record activities, outcomes, or responses to the station. However, the outcome from a station does not have to be something that is written on paper. Students may come away with a product such as a summary shared on a social media site (depending on your school's policies), or with such a product as a game, video, email, poster, diagram, blog, website article, or virtual demonstration.

- See the section "Technology Twists" in the introduction to this book. This provides a checklist of further suggestions for integrating technology into science literacy activities (pages 7 through 9).

Connecting to Standards

Keep literacy standards handy at all times. As you plan each station, identify standards that will be addressed. Purposely focus a station to strengthen a particular literacy skill or set of skills. The Standards-Connections charts on pages 10 through 16 identify Common Core State Standards and Next Generation Science Standards practices that are addressed by the general approach described in each station. However, the content and specific strategies you choose for a station will undoubtedly add other stan dards (from any set of standards) to the list for that station.

Scheduling and Organizing

Prepare a visual guide (such as following table) to help students move smoothly between stations. It is logical to have them rotate through stations in chronological order from where they initially begin. This means that you will need to start different students at different stations.

Guide to Science Stations

Broad Topic:		
Dates:		
Station Title	**Station Location**	**Group Schedule**
Station 1:		
Station 2:		
Station 3:		
Station 4:		
Station 5:		

SCIENCE STATION IDEAS

Note: After each station description, find sample forms, record sheets, and handouts to use with the science stations or to use as models for developing your own.

STATION #1   *Collage Capers*

Station Goal: to gather words and images that show or tell something about the concept or topic identified at the station

Supplies:

- old magazines
- product catalogs
- newspapers
- scissors
- glue sticks and tape
- large poster board
- copies of COLLAGE CAPERS Station Report for students (page 63)

- Each student contributes words, phrases, short sentences, and/or images to an all-class collage that communicates a particular message about a concept. By the time the last students finish at the station, the poster should be filled with messages that explain or depict the topic.

- Students can use the COLLAGE CAPERS Station Report to elaborate on some choices. Each student can explain a few of his or her choices to the group at the station.

After the Station:
Review the collage of one or more other groups who visited the station. Work together to craft a text message that evaluates how well the group's collage accomplished the purpose of the assignment. (If the group wishes, the message may compare the collage to or contrast it with a second collage.) Text this to one or more members of the other group so that someone from that group can respond with comments or differing opinions.

COLLAGE CAPERS Station Report

Station # _____ **Topic** _____ **Group #** _____ **Name** _____

Directions: For this activity, you will contribute to a class collage about the topic listed above. Use words, phrases, short sentences, and images that show or tell something that describes or demonstrates the topic. If specific words cannot be found in the magazines, newspapers, or catalogs, you can cut out individual letters to make the needed words.

Tasks:

1. In the chart below, briefly list or describe what you contributed to the collage. In the "Group" row, simply write the total number of each that your group contributed. Individual letters that make up specific words should be counted as one word.

Contributor	Words	Phrases or Sentences	Images
My Contributions			
My Group's Contributions (total number amount only)			

2. Choose two of your contributions and explain what they tell about the topic or how they help someone understand the concept.

_____

_____

_____

_____

_____

_____

_____

STATION #2 *Group Graffiti*

Station Goal: to help students and the teacher see the progression of students' knowledge about the broad multistation topic as they move through learning stations

Supplies:
- colored pencils
- markers
- crayons, and/or colored chalk
- medium-size poster board
- copies of GROUP GRAFFITI Station Report for students (page 65)

- Give each group of students a piece of poster board as they visit the station. Provide as many small- to medium-sized poster boards as the number of groups that will be visiting the stations. Write one group's number at the top of each poster. Each group visiting the station should also indicate their order in visiting (i.e., first group, second group, etc.).

- Students contribute "graffiti" to the poster board—adding phrases, quotes, words, diagrams, or pictures to depict their understanding of the topic.

- When about five minutes remain for this activity, go to this station and show graffiti posters made by the previous groups. Ask students to describe the progression of the graffiti (noticing how it may differ from first to second to third group, and so on.) Depending on how many posters they see, students may notice that the amount of graffiti increases as groups have been to other stations on this topic. The later groups have gained more knowledge from other stations. Of course, the first group will not be able to view other posters. Ask them to predict how the graffiti posters might be affected as a group progresses through other stations on this topic.

- Students can use the GROUP GRAFFITI Station Report to elaborate on some choices.

After the Station:
Select and synthesize several of the graffiti expressions into a visual map to show a key concept and supporting details.

GROUP GRAFFITI Station Report

Station # _____ Topic _____ Group # _____ Name _____

Our group came to the station _____ *(first, second, etc.).*

Directions: Write your group's number at the top of the page, along with the topic, your name, and the word first, second, third, etc. to tell the order in which your group visited the station. With about five minutes remaining with this activity, send a group member to get the teacher. For this activity, add drawings, words, sayings, and phrases to communicate your ideas of what the topic is about.

Tasks:

1. Circle the order of rotation listed below in which your group visited this station. Look at the posters from each group's graffiti that preceded your group. In the spaces below, list as much of the graffiti from your group and the other groups as you can.

1st Group	2nd Group	3rd Group	4th Group	5th Group	6th Group

2. What do you notice about the progression of the graffiti? What do you think is the reason for this?

If you are the first group to visit this station, what do you think the progression will look like as each group visits? Why?

_____

_____

_____

STATION #3   *Log On!*

Station Goal: to use Internet resources to apply or extend concepts from a science topic

> **Supplies:**
> - computers, pens or pencils
> - copies of LOG ON! Station Report for students (page 67)

- If enough computers are available, students can work in pairs at this station. Give them a web-based activity to gain some information that contributes understanding about the topic or displays concepts. You may choose to have students conduct a WebQuest, play an interactive game, search for content, blog about a question posed by you, create a cartoon or graphic organizer using downloadable software, or any other interactive online activity.

- Ask students to briefly describe (orally or in writing) what they did and what they learned by doing the activity. Students might also evaluate the website. Students can use the LOG ON! Station Report to show what they did and learned, and to evaluate the website or program.

After the Station:

Working as individuals or in pairs, choose one concept strengthened or understood through the Internet experience. Identify a position that could be argued related to that concept. Set up an email or Skype™ debate (depending on your school's policies) where students or pairs pass claims and reasons back and forth.

LOG ON! Station Report

Station # _____ **Topic** _____ **Group #** _____ **Name** _____

Directions: Follow the instructions at the station for an activity that uses the Internet.

Task: Complete the following report about the online activity you followed.

1. This is the URL of the site, program, or app we used:

2. These are the steps we followed:

3. These are the concepts encountered or used that are related to the science topic:

4. An important thing I learned about the science topic through this activity is:

5. Check one answer and explain:
   I _____ would or _____ would not recommend other students to use this site again because:

STATION #4 — Discovery Corner

Station Goals: to follow a discovery process to investigate a question, event, or concept; to describe what happens and what is learned

Supplies:
- resource materials and other supplies related to the assigned investigation
- copies of DISCOVERY CORNER Station Report for students (page 69)

- Pose a question or set up a situation with some statements. For example:
  What happens when you try to shine light through the five substances?
  What does this teach you?
  Which of these statements are true:
  > a. *The greater the mass of a ball, the faster it will accelerate down the inclined plane.*
  > b. *The smaller the size of a ball, the faster it will accelerate down the inclined plane.*
  > c. *The substance of which a ball is made makes no difference in its acceleration.*

- Provide all materials students will need to discover information or answers.

- After the investigation is complete, students can use the DISCOVERY CORNER Station Report to describe what they did, what they learned, and how it relates to the topic. Give the groups opportunities to share and demonstrate what they learned.

- **NOTE:** *The discovery process is a critical skill for science students. Include many discovery experiences in stations and your other instructional activities. Include at least one discovery station in every group of stations you design. Involve students in this task! Students will use a host of science, literacy, and creativity skills to design a discovery experience for a station (and write the instructions for other students).*

After the Station:
Visually display the outcome of the discovery process. Create a graph, model, table, or diagram on paper or with a digital app or online program.

DISCOVERY CORNER Station Report

Station # _____ **Topic** _____ **Group #** _____ **Name** _____

Directions: Follow the instructions at the station to work through a science investigation.

Task: When you finish the investigation, complete the items below to reflect on what you did and what you learned.

1. With this investigation, we wanted to find out:

2. These are the steps we followed:

3. Here is a summary of the results:

4. An important thing I learned from this investigation is:

5. Here is a way we could demonstrate to others what we learned:

STATION #5 — Hurrah for Nonfiction!

Station Goals: to use reference and other nonfiction materials to increase understanding of a topic; to use speaking skills to discuss the topic with others; to share information graphically; and to properly cite sources in writing

Supplies:

- reference and other nonfiction materials on the science topic
- copies of HURRAH FOR NONFICTION! Station Report for students (page 71)

- Visit your school library or media center or local public library. Collect as many resources as possible about the science topic you want students to explore. If a computer or other digital device is available that can access online articles, add a few good Internet sources to the collection. In all, there should be enough sources available so that each student in a group can read one or more items independently.

- Ask students to read their sources to find information that will help them understand the science topic or concept. Give them a designated amount of time to read the source. (Provide a timer, if possible.)

- After students read, each student has two to three minutes to share with the group what the source contributed to his or her understanding of the topic. Students can use the HURRAH FOR NONFICTION! Station Report to record citations and visually share information learned.

After the Station:

Students connect the science concept explored in the station to a real-life issue from current events. Create a mock news headline with a summarizing article to post on the class website or on a blog. Or record the headline and story on an audio file and upload a short blog (depending on your school's policies).

HURRAH FOR NONFICTION! Station Report

Station # _____ Topic _____ Group # _____ Name _____

Directions: Read or skim your nonfiction resource to gain as much understanding as you can about the topic.

Task:
Identify the source and present something you learned from it.

1. Write the citation for this source in MLA format (include the pages consulted):

2. Use the diagram to create a representation of something you learned:

Topic or Concept

Key idea I learned:	Key idea I learned:

Supporting Detail	Supporting Detail	Supporting Detail	Supporting Detail

STATION #6   *Quest for Questions*

Station Goal: to formulate good questions about what students hope to learn

Supplies:
- strips of cardstock for sentences (sentence strips)
- markers
- copies of QUEST FOR QUESTIONS Station Tasks sheet (page 73)

- The activity at this station is well suited as an introduction to a unit. Students can use the QUEST FOR QUESTIONS Station Tasks sheet to write questions about a science topic. The quest leads students to think about what they might learn or want to learn from the upcoming unit.

- Present a written or recorded introduction to an upcoming science unit. Each student writes two questions that he or she hopes will be answered during the unit. After questions are written, students share them with other group members to see if others may be able to answer their individual questions.

- Next, students work together with other group members to create one group question that encompasses the ideas of others or that members agree is the most relevant question from the group. A group member writes the question neatly on a sentence strip. Each student also writes this question on the QUEST FOR QUESTIONS Station Tasks sheet.

- The sentence strip is left where other students can see it, so that other groups will not develop the same question.

- After all groups have finished this activity, display the questions in the classroom. Refer to these throughout the unit as questions are answered from the learning activities. At the end of the unit, review all questions to determine how many were answered during the unit.

After the Station:
Students use a survey or interview format to find out how the station activity (forming questions) benefited others as they studied the topic. They can use an Internet survey program such as Survey Monkey, or prepare questions to "Ask the Experts" in video-taped interviews. (The experts are the other students.) In either case, they record and summarize the answers.

QUEST FOR QUESTIONS Station Tasks

Station # _____ **Topic** _____ **Group #** _____ **Name** _____

Directions: Think of questions about the topic that you hope will be answered as you study this unit. You'll share these questions with your group and work together to develop a group question. As you study the unit, watch and listen for the answers to your questions.

Tasks:

1. Write your two questions below.

A. _____

_____

_____

B. _____

_____

_____

2. Work with other group members to write one question about this topic that all group members agree should be answered. It may be a question posed by a group member or a question that combines questions from your group. Write the group question here:

_____

_____

_____

3. Select someone from the group to write the question neatly on a sentence strip. Leave your sentence strip on the table so that other groups visiting the station will not use the same question.

_____

_____

_____

STATION #7   Text Walk

Station Goal: increase skills in skimming science text for key details

Supplies:

- science text (chapter in textbook or other text students need to read, including digital or online text)
- questions for students to answer
- copies of TEXT WALK Student Question Sheet for students (page 75)

- Identify the text that students should read at the station and establish the amount of time students will be allotted to read the selection.

- Prepare a list of questions that relate to important ideas, facts, and concepts in the selected science text. Design questions that require students to use skimming skills to look for featured vocabulary, highlighted information, captions with images, headings, sub-headings, or concluding summaries. Create questions that students can answer with short explanations or details. You'll want students to gain insights into the science topic and deepen understandings of the concepts while they practice skimming. So pose questions that draw them to specific pages, sections, features, or paragraphs and that get at important facts or explanations—even if the approach is a trivia-style activity.

- Students "walk through" the text together, skimming, with the goal of answering as many questions as possible in the time allotted.

- As an option, students might contribute questions to the list. In this case, give them ample time to share their questions with group members so that other members can try to find the answers.

- You might also choose to have teacher- and student-designed questions. If students are required to design questions themselves, they should be given ample time to share their individual questions with group members so that others in their group can attempt to find the answers before leaving the station. Students may use the TEXT WALK Student Question Sheets to record their self-created questions and answers.

After the Station:

Students use mural paper, sidewalk chalk (outdoors), or mark up an old plastic tablecloth to create an actual path for a text walk. They write key ideas, facts, symbols, and phrases to represent visually what the text reveals as one walks through (skims through) the chapter. The finished product represents a summary of the skimmed text. Students could also do this as a virtual walk, creating the walkway on a tablet or other electronic device.

TEXT WALK Student Question Sheet

Station # _____ Topic _____ Group # _____ Name _____

Directions: Design a text walk from the text on the above topic.

Tasks:

1. Create questions for other students to use as they skim this material. Some of your questions can be trivia-type questions where readers must look at details in pictures or solve problems to find the answers. Spend half of the allotted time designing your text walk. Then trade papers with another pair in your group and use the rest of the time to answer their questions.

Page(s) if Applicable	QUESTIONS	ANSWERS
Example Pg. 356	What safety procedures are demonstrated by the girl in the picture as she performs the lab?	

2. Write two facts you learned as you created the text walk.

STATION #8   Watch, Learn, and Comment

Station Goals: to gain information from a visual format; to evaluate the presentation

Supplies:
- video clip and device for viewing
- copies of WATCH, LEARN, and COMMENT Station Report for students (page 77)

- Choose a brief video (such as a YouTube™ video segment or a selection from another source that permits free classroom display) that relates to the topic of the stations.

- Provide instructions for one or more tasks students can complete after watching the video. You might ask them to list important facts discussed, to summarize the information in the video, to identify and explain terminology used, or to describe or diagram an important concept that was shown. Or, you could provide questions for them to answer or statements that they'll mark true or false as they watch the video.

- Students can use the WATCH, LEARN, and COMMENT Report Sheet or other similar guide to watching the video.

- You also might also ask the students to evaluate the content and presentation or to compare this video clip to another one on the same topic.

After the Station:
Students design a rubric to use for the evaluation of a video clip. They should begin by identifying categories for evaluation and criteria to match varying levels of performance for each category. They can develop a scoring system to accompany the criteria. When completed, students use their own rubric to evaluate video clips.

WATCH, LEARN, and COMMENT Station Report

Station # _____ **Topic** _____ **Group #** _____ **Name** _____

Directions: View the video segment _____. While viewing the video, complete Task 1. When the video is finished, complete Tasks 2 and 3.

Tasks:

1. Briefly summarize the most important or surprising thing you learned from the video.

2. Draw a memorable image from a screen or section. Describe what you learned from the scene you chose to draw.

3. Explain what the video did well (or did not do well) to communicate the main message or concept.

_____

_____

_____

_____

_____

_____

STATION #9   *Virtual Lab*

Station Goal: to simulate a laboratory experience when a hands-on lab experience is not available

Supplies:

- computers
- copies of the VIRTUAL LAB Station Report for students (page 79)

- Take advantage of virtual labs. There are many free downloadable experiences for students. Many of the experiments can be performed in a 20-minute station session, most are interactive, and they require no equipment. Explore such sites as www.vlabs.co.in, www.virtuallabs.nmsu.edu, www.chemcollective.org, and www.mhhe.com/biosci/genbio/virtual_labs_2K8.

- Choose and assign a virtual lab at the station. Give students the URL for the lab.

- Provide students who need help navigating and using the site with a way to get assistance from the teacher or another student or helper.

- Provide a study guide or reporting sheet where students can describe the lab and what they learned. (See the VIRTUAL LAB Report Sheet.)

After the Station:

A natural extension of this activity is one where students design and create their own virtual lab to investigate a question or teach a concept. This will necessitate careful planning, gathering materials, identifying step-by-step procedures, practicing the process, filming the process, and posting the results.

VIRTUAL LAB Station Report

Station # _____ **Topic** _____ **Group #** _____ **Name** _____

Directions: Watch the virtual lab at URL: _____.

Task: When you finish the investigation, complete the items below to reflect on what you did and what you learned.

1. With this investigation, we wanted to find out:

2. These are the steps we followed:

3. Here is a summary of the results:

4. An important thing I learned from this investigation is:

5. Here is a way we could demonstrate to others what we learned:

STATION #10   *Concept Connection*

Station Goal: to understand, explain, and show connections between concepts within a broad science topic

Supplies:

- 12-inch squares of poster board, felt, or foam core
- permanent markers
- tape
- scissors
- large safety pins
- string
- copies of CONCEPT CONNECTION Station Report for students (page 81)

- Choose a set of concepts that make up a science unit. (For example, you might identify the following for a unit on electricity: *electrical charge, electric circuits, Coulomb's Law, electric force, batteries or electric cells, conductors and insulators, resistance, voltage, electrical current, static electricity,* and *electromagnetism.*)

- Write each concept on a square. (Leave several blank squares in the station.)

- Students will work together to make choices about connecting two or three concepts. They can actually connect the squares with large safety pins or string to group them together and hang or otherwise display. Include instructions in the station that the students are to explain or show how these concepts are connected. They may use the CONCEPT CONNECTION Station Report to record their explanations. If any students in the group disagree, they can use blank squares to create and write about different combinations of concepts.

- If there is time, students can include a second task of connecting the chosen concepts to real life situations, events, applications, and uses. They can show these relationships by writing phrases on other squares and connecting them to the joined concepts.

After the Station:
Students work in their station groups to make a jigsaw puzzle that connects some of the concepts from the topic studied. For puzzle pieces, use poster board, foam core, or other sturdy material. The puzzle, when assembled, should connect subtopics to a main topic or details to support a key concept.

CONCEPT CONNECTION Station Report

Station # _____ **Topic** _____ **Group #** _____ **Name** _____

Directions: Read the concepts that are identified on the squares. Discuss ways that some of these concepts are connected to each other. Identify two or three concepts that you agree are connected to each other. Connect the squares with string, safety pins, or some other fastener.

Tasks:

1. Name the concepts _____

_____

_____

2. Draw a diagram or write an explanation to show how these concepts connect to each another.

3. Think of at least two ways that these concepts are part of a real-life event, situation, or use. Write phrases on other squares and connect them to the concept squares. Briefly describe your ideas here.

STATION #11   *Station Evaluation*

Station Goals: to analyze and evaluate the usefulness, value, and effectiveness of a station; to make suggestions about further use or development of a station

Supplies:
- any science station
- copies of STATION EVALUATION Form for students (page 83)

- Create and use such a form or process as found on the STATION EVALUATION Form. Students use this to evaluate a station at the end of their experience with it. This will give valuable feedback to the teacher for improving instructional practices. In addition, this process gives students a voice in and ownership of their learning experiences.

- Give students opportunities to evaluate several science stations throughout the year. It is not necessary for every student to evaluate every station; but the teacher (or whoever designed a station) will benefit from some feedback on each one.

After the Station:
Students work together to summarize the station evaluation in 144 characters or fewer and assign one group member to tweet the summary to the teacher.

STATION EVALUATION Form

Station # _____ **Topic** _____ **Group #** _____ **Name** _____

Directions: Review and reflect on a science station that you have completed.

Task: Complete the form to give your evaluation of the station.

1. Describe the purpose of the station.

2. Summarize what you learned from completing the station.

3. What was best about the station? (What did it offer that was most effective in helping you learn about the topic?)

4. What new ideas or questions did you gain from completing the tasks at this station?

5. What would you do differently to the design or tasks in this station? Why?

STATION #12   Design-a-Station

Station Goal: to give students the learning experience of designing science stations

Supplies:

• copies of PLAN FOR DESIGNING A STATION for students (page 85)

• During any school year in your science class, give students opportunities to design their own stations. They can work in small groups, or some students might want to craft individual plans. This is an excellent way for students to conduct independent learning on a topic (they'll need to know plenty in order to design a good station for other students) or to deepen their understandings of a topic they have already studied.

• You can set up a station with resources, instructions, and technological devices for students to use in planning stations. Use a form such as the PLAN FOR DESIGNING A STATION as a starting point for students to sketch out the components and steps for making and using a station.

After the Station:

Students design a feedback tool or process for the station designs. A pair of students can review each design plan and use the tool to respond to the designers. This will help individuals or groups fine-tune their plans for learning stations.

PLAN FOR DESIGNING A STATION

Name _____

The topic:

Concepts or processes the station will teach, reinforce, or assess understanding of:

Purpose of the station:

Materials needed:

How you'll make the station appealing to students:

Steps students will need to follow:

Chapter 3
Mathematics Literacy Strategies

Mathematics is ever present in the science classroom. To expand and deepen skills of science literacy, students need serious practice in mathematics literacy as well. Students working with science projects, processes, and assignments will be called on to understand mathematical language over and over as they:

- read texts, inquiry steps, assignments, instructions, or assessments that include mathematical concepts processes and terms;

- take, calculate, synthesize, and record measurements;

- solve real-world problems, investigate hypotheses, carry out experiments and investigations, gather, record, and compute results, and evaluate results; and

- write, discuss, and present findings and statistics using graphs, charts, and physical and virtual models.

Students can become overwhelmed with the multiple mathematical formulas, variable symbols, and measurement units used in science. This chapter contains a set of strategies to build understandings of concepts that are intricately connected to formulas and calculations. When students understand the variables in the formulas as concepts that can be defined and investigated, and when they learn to identify the units that are used for particular variables, they'll grow by leaps and bounds in their abilities to master mathematics!

Using the Tools, Formulas, and Strategies

Review Lessons A, B, C: This chapter begins with three review lessons (pages 91 through 93) to help teach or reinforce the language of the formulas and the relationships between the variables and measurement units in formulas. Use these as mini-lessons or formative assessments before asking students to use the formulas.

Tools A and B: Two tools offer help and support as students tackle any science problem that involves one of the topics in this chapter. One is an overview of the formulas. Students will refer to this often as they work with the concepts in this chapter. The other is the "Triangle Tool"—a handy aide for teaching any three-variable formula and rearranging it to solve for any of the three variables.

Strategy Sheets 1-15: Fifteen strategy sheets take the mystery out of using these formulas. Each sheet allows students to rearrange the basic formula into a form needed to solve a problem. The rewritten formulas become part of the student's record, and the same sheet can be used many times for similar problems.

Use each of the strategy sheets as a tool for teaching the related concept. For example, as students learn about **density,** they can begin right away to apply the concept by investigating real examples. Use the Density Calculations (page 97), along with the Triangle Tool (page 95). Work through the formula explanation and the sample problem to identify each variable and identify which variable in the density formula the problem-solver is asked to find.

After a lesson with each of these strategy pages, students can use them repeatedly for other problems. These work well with student pairs or small groups.

Moving Beyond the Calculation Tasks

Once students have had lessons on these calculation strategies and practiced turning the formulas around to suit the individual problems, they'll be ready to soar in their use of these formulas. Have students keep the review lessons, the formula overview (Tool A), the Triangle Tool sheet (Tool B), and the strategy sheets (pages 96 through 110) in a binder or portfolio or in an electronic form on a computer. They'll use these sheets until they are tattered (a good reason to keep them electronically)!

Urge students to watch for real-life scenarios and situations where they can apply their problem-solving skills and understandings of these 15 concepts. Offer extra-credit or challenge problems for continued use of the formulas.

Students can scan current news stories online or track down online problems about acceleration, density, electric current, or any of the other concepts in the chapter. They can work individually or in pairs to create problems for other students to solve.

As students solve more problems and practice using the formula rearrangements, they will come to understand the concepts more deeply. They can create a tutorial video or learning station to teach any or all of these calculation processes to other students. They might combine tutorials of different kinds into a blog or website (depending on your school's policies) for subsequent classes or students at a beginning level.

Differentiating Mathematical Literacy Tasks

In addition to different experiences and abilities with mathematics-related lessons, students in your science classroom will have different comfort levels with mathematics. Symbols and formulas are fun for some students; others get "brain freeze" when they see a Periodic Table or the formula for peroxide. Here are a few suggestions for differentiation to improve mathematics literacy in your science classroom:

- Modify processes that require complex mathematical literacy skills. Prepare assignments with different choices or levels for tasks.

- Prepare tools, such as those found on pages 94 and 95 of this chapter, to help students tackle tricky science calculations. When students have completed these review and strategy sheets, they have half their work done on upcoming problems. This greatly reduces stress and helps to scaffold struggling students to success. The formulas are already flipped and recorded in plain writing; students don't have to fret about how to find solutions.

- Break skills, concepts, and processes into small chunks. Plan and carry out fun mini-lessons on concepts and processes that use mathematics. Tackle these in short periods of time with active, relevant tasks that have a high rate of success. (For example, for 10 minutes, examine different electrical appliances to find labels or information about the amount of power they use. Or do a quick survey of inherited traits in the classroom and show the mathematical results on a graph or table.)

- Make available charts, lists, graphical explanations, and study guides. Students should feel that they have help at their fingertips at all times to decipher tasks and texts that require mathematics literacy. Give them a printed glossary of relevant mathematics-science formulas, abbreviations, acronyms, and symbols. Provide graphic organizers or step-by-step guides for solving problems.

- Games and scavenger hunts can allow for different answers or outcomes, adapting to numerous learners. Play games with the Periodic Table, chemical formulas, and symbols. Send students on scavenger hunts for objects or situations that can connect to a symbol. Match common items with formulas. Find things in the classroom that contain an element (identified by its symbol).

- Pair students to translate or create cryptic messages containing symbols or formulas. Give lists of mathematics-connected items with different levels of difficulty or complexity, geared to the students.

- Stop for short measurement breaks: Practice measuring with all kinds of units in real-life situations. This gives a variety of measurement experiences that will span interest and ability levels. (For example, before students work with formulas that use different units, they must be familiar with the individual units. Measure elapsed time, mass of objects, volume of liquids and solids, change in temperature over a period of time, or change in speed over a period of time.)

- Translate mathematical labels, formulas, or symbols into words. If cell phones are available in the classroom, students can tweet, text, or instant message the word translations to classmates, who must translate the words back into the mathematical language. Offer a range of difficulties and complexities of messages to be translated.

Connecting to Technology

- Technology offers many pathways to improving mathematics literacy in science. Visit reliable science-related websites*; the articles and information can be wonderful sources of topics and data for developing science math problems. On their computers and phones, students can find free and educational apps for drawing geometric figures, designing models, solving equations, and working formulas. They can also use a variety of good-quality tutorial programs to learn science or math concepts and solve problems relevant to science. For example, visit the Khan Academy online for help with all sorts of science and mathematics concepts at www.khanacademy.org. See also, Wolfram Alpha at www.wolframalpha.com/educators/.

  *www.nasa.gov; www.noaa.gov; http://kids.nationalgeographic.com; www.exploratorium.edu; https://student.societyforscience.org/sciencenews-students/; www.brainpop.com/science; www.si.edu

- In addition, see the section "Technology Twists" in the introduction to this book for a checklist of technology connections to help you integrate technology into science literacy activities (pages 7 through 9).

Connecting to Standards

The review lessons, tools, and strategies in this chapter naturally align with several science, literacy, and mathematics standards. These are identified in the Standards Connections charts on pages 10 through 16. However, as students read, write, listen, speak, and think through presentations and texts on other, content-specific science topics, you'll find that the coverage of standards ranges far beyond science and mathematics literacy. Many domain-specific and cross-cutting concepts standards are also covered. Keep your standards for science, mathematics, and literacy handy at all times. Note which standards are addressed with each lesson or assessment. You and your students will be amazed at how many literacy standards are practiced within those science-mathematics activities!

Variable? Or Unit?

Variable: a factor that can be measured

Unit: the specific measurement of a variable

Directions: Use the terms and symbols in the word box. Decide if each one is a *variable* or a *unit of measurement*. Mark it V (variable) or U (unit of measurement).

1. acceleration _____

2. amps _____

3. density _____

4. distance _____

5. energy _____

6. force _____

7. grams _____

8. gravity _____

9. heat _____

10. joules _____

11. mass _____

12. meters _____

13. momentum _____

14. newtons _____

15. ohms _____

16. potential energy _____

17. power _____

18. resistance _____

19. seconds _____

20. temperature _____

21. time _____

22. velocity _____

23. volts _____

24. volume _____

25. watts _____

26. work _____

27. specific heat _____

28. ΔT _____

29. pressure _____

30. λ _____

31. electric current _____

32. Ω _____

33. E_k _____

Variable Match

Directions: Match each term in the word box to its definition or description below.

acceleration	calorie	resistance	volts	c
density	heat	temperature	work	E_k
distance	momentum	time	g	Q
energy	power	velocity	p	ΔT
force	potential energy	volume	I	λ

1. _____ speed in a given direction

2. _____ change in velocity over a period of time

3. _____ symbol for momentum

4. _____ stored energy

5. _____ push or pull on an object

6. _____ symbol for current

7. _____ ability to do work

8. _____ change in temperature

9. _____ electromotive force units

10. _____ mass per unit of volume

11. _____ symbol for heat

12. _____ measure of thermal energy

13. _____ symbol for wavelength

14. _____ opposes electricity flow

15. _____ units are seconds

16. _____ kinetic energy

17. _____ symbol for specific heat

18. _____ 9.8 m/s^2

19. _____ common units are meters

20. _____ transfer of thermal energy

21. _____ amount of space taken up

22. _____ force applied over distance

23. _____ a unit for measuring heat

24. _____ rate of doing work

Name _____

Unit Match

Directions: Use the terms and symbols in the Word Bank and match each with its appropriate variable. Some will be used multiple times for various variables.

amps	m/s	seconds	cm3
Celsius	m/s²	volts	mL
grams	meters	watts	g/mL
kg·m/s	newtons	Ω	
joules	ohms	A	

1. _____ velocity

2. _____ force

3. _____ momentum

4. _____ work

5. _____ current

6. _____ temperature

7. _____ mass

8. _____ power

9. _____ potential energy

10. _____ time

11. _____ & _____ resistance

12. _____ electromotive force

13. _____ distance

14. _____ density

15. _____ & _____ volume

16. _____ & _____ current

17. _____ heat

18. _____ electrical power

19. _____ acceleration

20. _____ kinetic energy

TOOL A

Mathematical Formulas Commonly Used in Science

Sample word problems and necessary formula rearrangements for the following formulas can be found on pages 96 through 110.

Formulas	Abbreviations	Units
Acceleration = change in velocity (m/s)**/time** (s)	$a = \Delta v/t$	m/s^2
Density = mass (g)**/volume** (mL or cm³)	$D = m/v$	g/mL or g/cm^3
Electrical energy = power (kw) **x time** (h)	$E = Pt$	kilowatt-hours
Electrical power = volts (v) **x current** (A)	$P = VI$	watts (W)
Force = mass (kg) **x acceleration** (m/s²)	$F = ma$	newtons (N)
Heat = mass (g) **x specific heat** (J/g°C) **x change in temperature** (°C)	$Q = mc\Delta T$	joules (J)
Kinetic energy = ½ mass (kg) **x velocity²**(m/s)	$E_k = \frac{1}{2}mv^2$	joules (J)
Momentum = mass (kg) **x velocity** (m/s)	$p = mv$	kg x m/s
(Ohm's Law) Current = volts (V)**/resistance** (ohms (Ω))	$I = V/R$	amps (A)
Potential energy = mass (kg) **x gravity** (m/s²) **x height** (m)	$E_p = mgh$	joules (J)
Power = work (J)**/time** (s)	$P = W/t$	Watt (W)
Speed (Velocity) = distance (m)**/time** (s)	$v = d/t$	m/s
Volume = length (m or cm) **x width** (m or cm) **x height** (m or cm) (cm x cm x cm = cm³)	$V = lwh$	cm^3 or m^3
Wave speed = frequency (Hz) **x wavelength** (m)	$v = f\lambda$	m/s
Work = force (N) **x distance** (m)	$W = fd$	joules (J)

The Triangle Tool

This is a valuable little tool for solving formulas. The visual model makes it easier for students to manipulate variables when they need to rearrange a formula in order to find a different variable that would be found in the formula's original form. Share copies of this example with students. They'll use this triangle over and over!

Example: $a = \Delta v/t$

$\Delta v = a \times t$

$t = \dfrac{\Delta v}{a}$

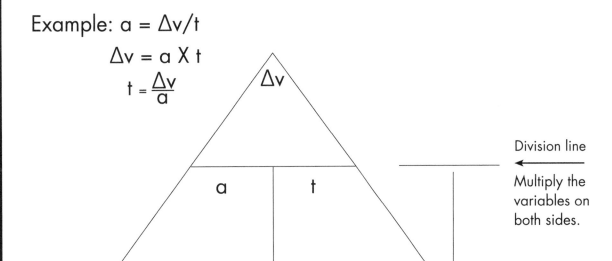

Division line

Multiply the variables on both sides.

Note that the horizontal line beneath the small top triangle indicates division.

The vertical line on the bottom indicates multiplication.

In this example, the X stands for "times" or multiplication.

For this example, the triangle allows you to arrange, rearrange, and visualize a way to find each of the variables:

To find **a** (acceleration), divide **Δv** (change in velocity) by time **t** (time).

To find **Δv** (change in velocity), multiply **a** (acceleration) by **t** (time).

To find t (time), divide **Δv** (change in velocity) by **a** (acceleration).

Acceleration Calculations

Acceleration is speeding up, slowing down, or changing direction; it is a change in velocity over a period of time.

Velocity is speed in a given direction.

Change in velocity is final velocity – initial velocity **(v_f minus v_i) or Δv**

Acceleration = <u>Change in Velocity (m/s)</u>
                              Time (s)
Meters per second squared (m/s^2) are the units used to express acceleration.

> **Use the formula given for acceleration and rearrange the variables to determine the formulas for the other variables in the original formula. Include the appropriate units.**
>
> **a = Δv/t   Change in Velocity =   Total Time =**

Sample word problem used in the chart below:
From the start of the race, the car's speed after 5 seconds was 20 m/s. What was the car's acceleration during this time?

Place a question mark under the variable for which you are solving. Place the given numbers from the word problem in the appropriate boxes. Be sure to include appropriate units in the solution column. Use the empty rows for solving other problems.

Acceleration (m/s^2)	Final Velocity (m/s)	Initial Velocity (m/s)	Change in Velocity (m/s)	Time (s)	Problem	Solution
Example: **?** m/s^2	20 m/s	0 m/s	20 m/s	5 s	a = <u>20 – 0</u> = <u>20 m/s</u> 5 5 s	4 m/s^2

Density Calculations

Density is mass per unit of volume. The density of water is 1 gram per milliliter. Anything with a density greater than one g/mL will sink in water. Anything with a density less than one g/mL will float in water.

Mass is the amount of matter in an object, and **volume** is the amount of space an object takes up.

Density = mass (g) **per unit of volume** (mL)

Grams per milliliter or cubic centimeter (g/mL or g/cm³) are units used to express density. (A milliliter equals 1 cubic centimeter.)

> **Use the formula given for density and rearrange the variables to determine the formulas for the other variables in the original formula. Include the appropriate units.**
>
> **D = m/V**   **Mass =**   **Volume =**

Sample word problem used in the chart below:
If a moon rock has a density of 2 g/mL and a volume of 8 mL, what is its mass?

Place a question mark under the variable for which you are solving. Place the numbers from the given word problem in the appropriate boxes. Be sure to include appropriate units in the solution column. Use the empty rows for solving other problems.

Density (g/mL or g/cm³)	Mass (g)	Volume (mL or cm³)	Problem	Solution
Example: 2 g/mL	?	8 mL	m = 2 x 8	16 g

Electrical Energy Calculations

Electrical energy is carried by the flow of electrons through a circuit. It is the movement of electric charges. Electric companies are paid for the amount of electrical energy we use in our homes.

Electrical energy = power (kW) **x time** (h)

Kilowatt hours (kilowatts times hours or kWh) are the units used to express electrical energy. Note that there are 1,000 watts in a kilowatt.

> **Use the formula given for electrical energy and rearrange the variables to determine the formulas for the other variables in the original formula. Include the appropriate units.**
>
> **E = Pt   Power =   Time =**

Sample word problem used in the chart below:
Calculate the electrical energy used by a 12-watt light bulb over 72 hours.

Place a question mark under the variable for which you are solving. Place the numbers from the given word problem in the appropriate boxes. Be sure to include appropriate units in the solution column. Use the empty rows for solving other problems.

Electrical energy (kWh)	Power (kW)	Time (h)	Problem	Solution
Example: **?** kWh	12 W	72 h	E = 12 x 72	864 Watt hours = 0.864 kWh

Electrical Power Calculations

Electrical power is the rate at which electrical energy is used or transferred. ***Current*** is the flow of electrical energy through a circuit. Current is measured in **amps,** but the symbol for current is "I." ***Volts*** supply the "push" that causes the current to flow.

Electrical power = volts (V) **x current** (I) *measured in amps (A)*

Watts are used to measure electrical power, but generally the measurement is expressed in ***kilowatts*** (thousands of watts).

> **Use the formula given for electrical power and rearrange the variables to determine the formulas for the other variables in the original formula. Include the appropriate units.**
>
> **P = VI**   **Current (I) =**   **Volts =**

Sample word problem used in the chart below:
A device connected to 240 V runs 31 amps of current. How much power does it use?

Place a question mark under the variable for which you are solving. Place the numbers from the given word problem in the appropriate boxes. Be sure to include appropriate units in the solution column. Use the empty rows for solving other problems.

Electrical Power (kW)	Current (I) (amps)	Volts (V)	Problem	Solution
Example: **?** kW	31 A	240 V	P = 31 x 240	7,440 W = 7.440 kW

Force Calculations

Force is defined as a push or pull on an object. A combination of all the forces acting on an object is the **net force.** Balanced forces yield a net force of zero. **Mass** is the amount of matter in an object, and **acceleration** is a change in velocity over time.

Force = mass (kg) **x acceleration** (m/s²)

Newtons (N) are the units used to express force. One newton equals 1 kg x 1 m/s².

> **Use the formula given for force and rearrange the variables to determine the formulas for the other variables in the original formula. Include the appropriate units.**
>
> **F = ma   Mass =   Acceleration =**

Sample word problem used in the chart below:
If an object has a net force of 21,000 N and a mass of 3,500 kg, what is the object's acceleration?

Place a question mark under the variable for which you are solving. Place the numbers from the given word problem in the appropriate boxes. Be sure to include appropriate units in the solution column. Use the empty rows for solving other problems.

Force (N)	Mass (kg)	Acceleration (m/s²)	Problem	Solution
Example: 21,000 N	3500 kg	**?** m/s²	F = $\frac{21,000}{3,500}$	6 m/s²

Heat Calculations

Heat is the transfer of thermal energy. The symbol for heat is "Q." **Mass** is the amount of matter in an object. **Specific heat** is the amount of heat required to raise the temperature of 1 gram of a substance by 1 degree Celsius. It is expressed in joules per gram of mass times temperature in Celsius. **Change in temperature** is the final temperature minus the initial temperature.

Heat = mass (g) x specific heat (c or J/(g•°C) x change in temperature (°C)

Joules (J) are the units used to express heat (Q).

> **Use the formula given for heat (Q) and rearrange the variables to determine the formulas for the other variables in the original formula. Include the appropriate units.**
>
> **Q = mcΔT   Mass =   Specific Heat =   ΔTemperature =**

Sample word problem used in the chart below:
The specific heat of water is 4.18 J/g•°C. If the temperature of 80 grams of water rose from 35 °C to 92 °C, what was the amount of heat absorbed into the water?

Place a question mark under the variable for which you are solving. Place the numbers from the given word problem in the appropriate boxes. Be sure to include appropriate units in the solution column. Use the empty rows for solving other problems.

Heat (Q) (J)	Mass (g)	Specific Heat (J/g•°C)	Final Temp. (°C)	Initial Temp. (°C)	Change in Temp. (°C)	Problem	Solution
Example: **?** J	80 g	4.18 J/g•°C	92 °C	35 °C	92 – 35 = 57 °C	Q = 80 x 4.18 x 57	19,060.8 J

Kinetic Energy Calculations

Kinetic energy is defined as the energy of motion. **Mass** is the amount of matter in an object, and **velocity** is speed in a given direction.

Kinetic energy = ½ mass (kg) **x velocity²** (m/s)

Joules (J) are the units used to express kinetic energy.

> **Use the formula given for kinetic energy and rearrange the variables to determine the formulas for the other variables in the original formula. Include the appropriate units.**
> $$E_k = \tfrac{1}{2} mv^2 \qquad \text{Mass} = \qquad \text{Velocity} =$$

Sample word problem used in the chart below:
A ball with a mass of 0.02 kg rolls down a hill at a velocity of 4 m/s. What is the ball's kinetic energy?

Place a question mark under the variable for which you are solving. Place the numbers from the given word problem in the appropriate boxes. Be sure to include appropriate units in the solution column. Use the empty rows for solving other problems.

Kinetic energy (J)	Mass (kg)	Velocity (m/s)	Problem	Solution
Example: **?** J	0.05 kg	6 m/s	$E_k = \tfrac{1}{2}\,(0.05) \times 6^2 =$ 0.025 X 36	0.9 J

WORD-PROBLEM STRATEGY #8   Name _____

Momentum Calculations

Momentum is the product of an object's mass and its velocity. The symbol for momentum is "p."
Mass is the amount of matter in an object, and **velocity** is speed in a given direction.

Momentum = mass (kg) **x velocity** (m/s)

Kilogram meters (kilograms times meters) per second (kg · m/s) are the units used to express momentum.

> **Use the formula given for momentum and rearrange the variables to determine the formulas for the other variables in the original formula. Include the appropriate units.**
>
> **p = mv**   **Mass =**   **Velocity =**

Sample word problem used in the chart below:
A rock with a mass of 0.04 kg has a momentum of 0.112 kg·m/s. What is the rock's velocity?

Place a question mark under the variable for which you are solving. Place the numbers from the given word problem in the appropriate boxes. Be sure to include appropriate units in the solution column. Use the empty rows for solving other problems.

Momentum (p) (kg·m/s)	Mass (kg)	Velocity (m/s)	Problem	Solution
Example: 0.112 kg·m/s	0.04 kg	**?** m/s	p = $\frac{0.112}{0.04}$	2.8 m/s

Ohm's Law Calculations

Ohm's Law shows the relationship among current, volts, and resistance in an electric circuit. ***Current*** is the flow of electric charges, ***volts*** supply the "push" for the charges to flow, and ***resistance*** is opposition to the flow of electricity. The symbol for current is "I." The symbol for resistance is the omega sign (Ω). Resistance is measured in ohms.

Current = volts (V) **per unit of resistance** (ohms) (Ω)

Amperes (amps, or A) are the units used to express current.

> **Use the formula given for current (I) and rearrange the variables to determine the formulas for the other variables in the original formula. Include the appropriate units.**
>
> **I = V/R   Volts =   Resistance =**

Sample word problem used in the chart below:

A small toy uses two AA batteries, which add up to 3 volts. The toy's circuit has a resistance of 12 Ω. What amount of current is used?

Place a question mark under the variable for which you are solving. Place the numbers from the given word problem in the appropriate boxes. Be sure to include appropriate units in the solution column. Use the empty rows for solving other problems.

Current (I) (amps)	Volts (V)	Resistance (Ω) (ohms)	Problem	Solution
Example: **?** A	3 V	12 Ω	I = $\frac{3}{12}$	0.25 A

Potential Energy Calculations

Potential energy is stored energy. The types of potential energy include chemical, elastic, and gravitational. We will use **gravitational potential energy** (GPE) for these calculations. **Mass** is the amount of matter in an object. The letter g stands for the acceleration due to Earth's gravity, which is 9.8 m/s^2. **Height** is the distance the object is raised above the ground.

Potential energy = mass (kg) **x g** (m/s^2) **x height** (h)

Joules are the units used to express potential energy.

> **Use the formula given for potential energy and rearrange the variables to determine the formulas for the other variables in the original formula. Include the appropriate units.**
>
> $E_p = mgh$ **Mass =**   **Height =**

Sample word problem used in the chart below:

What is the potential energy of a diver who has a mass of 56 kg and is diving from a height of 7 meters?

Place a question mark under the variable for which you are solving. Place the numbers from the given word problem in the appropriate boxes. Be sure to include appropriate units in the solution column. Use the empty rows for solving other problems.

Potential Energy (J)	Mass (kg)	g (m/s^2)	Height (h)	Problem	Solution
Example: **?** J	56 kg	9.8 m/s^2	7 m	GPE = 56 X 9.8 X 7	3,841.6 J

Power Calculations

Power is the rate of doing work. **Work** is force applied over a distance. We use a capital W to symbolize the work variable, but don't get confused—W is *also* the abbreviation for watt, the unit for power.

Power = work (J) per unit of time (s)

Watts (or *kilowatts*) are the units used to express power.

> **Use the formula given for power and rearrange the variables to determine the formulas for the other variables in the original formula. Include the appropriate units.**
>
> ### P = W/t   Work =   Time =

Sample word problem used in the chart below:
How much work can a 650-watt motor do in 1 hour (1 hour = 3,600 seconds)?

Place a question mark under the variable for which you are solving. Place the numbers from the given word problem in the appropriate boxes. Be sure to include appropriate units in the solution column. Use the empty rows for solving other problems.

Power (watt)	Work (J)	Time (s)	Problem	Solution
Example: 650 W	**?** J	3,600 s	P = 650 X 3,600	2,340,000 J

Speed or Velocity Calculations

Speed and velocity are generally used as interchangeable concepts. Speed is distance traveled over a unit of time, whereas velocity is the distance traveled over a unit of time in a certain direction. In other words, velocity is speed in a given direction. Both are calculated using the same formula.

Speed (Velocity) = distance (m) **per unit of time** (s)

Meters per second (m/s) are the units commonly used in the sciences to express speed and velocity.

> **Use the formula given for speed/velocity and rearrange the variables to determine the formulas for the other variables in the original formula. Include the appropriate units.**
>
> **S = d/t   Distance =   Time =**

Sample word problem used in the chart below:

A baby crawled 5 m across the floor at a speed of 0.833 m/s. How long did it take the baby to travel this distance?

Place a question mark under the variable for which you are solving. Place the numbers from the given word problem in the appropriate boxes. Be sure to include appropriate units in the solution column. Use the empty rows for solving other problems.

Speed or Velocity (m/s)	Distance (m)	Time (s)	Problem	Solution
Example: 0.0833 m/s	5 m	**?** s	t= $\frac{5}{0.0833}$	60 s

Volume Calculations

Volume is the amount of space an object takes up. Generally, if the volume being measured is a liquid or of an irregularly shaped object, the units are liters (L) or milliliters (mL). When measuring the volume of a regularly shaped object, use the formula shown below.

Volume = length (m or cm) **x width** (m or cm) **x height** (m or cm) (cm **x** cm **x** cm = cm^3)

Cubic centimeters or cubic meters (cm^3 or m^3) are some of the units that express volume. These are derived from multiplying length **x** width **x** height.

(cm **x** cm **x** cm = cm^3 or m **x** m **x** m = m^3)

> **Use the formula given for volume and rearrange the variables to determine the formulas for the other variables in the original formula. Include the appropriate units.**
>
> **V = lwh   Length =   Width =   Height =**

Sample word problem used in the chart below:
What is the volume of a box that has a length of 4.3 cm, a width of 7 cm, and a height of 3 cm?

Place a question mark under the variable for which you are solving. Place the numbers from the given word problem in the appropriate boxes. Be sure to include appropriate units in the solution column. Use the empty rows for solving other problems.

Volume (cm³ or m³)	Length (cm)	Width (cm)	Height (cm)	Problem	Solution
Example: **?** cm³	4.3 cm	7 cm	3 cm	V = 4.3 X 7 X 3	90.3 cm³

Wave Speed Calculations

Wave speed is the distance a wave travels in a period of time. **Wave frequency** is the number of wave crests that pass a point in a second. Frequency is measured in **hertz** (Hz), which means 1 wave cycle per second. **Wavelength** is the distance between two wave crests. The **Lambda** (λ) is the symbol used for wavelength.

Wave speed = frequency (Hz) x wavelength (m)

Meters per second (m/s) are the units used to express wave speed.

> **Use the formula given for wave speed and rearrange the variables to determine the formulas for the other variables in the original formula. Include the appropriate units.**
>
> **v = fλ   Frequency =   Wavelength (λ) =**

Sample word problem used in the chart below:

15 wave crests pass a buoy in 20 seconds, which makes the wave frequency 0.75 Hz. If the wave is traveling 12 m/s, what is the wavelength of each wave?

Place a question mark under the variable for which you are solving. Place the numbers from the given word problem in the appropriate boxes. Be sure to include appropriate units in the solution column. Use the empty rows for solving other problems.

Wave Speed (m/s)	Frequency (Hz)	Wavelength (m)	Problem	Solution
Example: 12 m/s	0.75 Hz	**?** m	λ = $\frac{12}{0.75}$	16 m

Work Calculations

Work is force applied over a distance. **Force** is a push or pull on an object, and is measured in newtons.

$$\textbf{Work = force (N) x distance (m)}$$

Joules (J) are the units used to express work.

> **Use the formula given for work and rearrange the variables to determine the formulas for the other variables in the original formula. Include the appropriate units.**
>
> **W = Fd   Force =   Distance =**

Sample word problem used in the chart below:
The work done on an object was 243 J. How much force was needed to move the object 3 meters?

Place a question mark under the variable for which you are solving. Place the numbers from the given word problem in the appropriate boxes. Be sure to include appropriate units in the solution column. Use the empty rows for solving other problems.

Work (J)	Force (N)	Distance (m)	Problem	Solution
Example: 243 J	? N	3 m	F = $\dfrac{243}{3}$	81 N

Science Vocabulary

The following lists include many, but certainly not all, the terms that will help to build a healthy science vocabulary for upper intermediate and secondary students. Words, however, are not the whole picture of science literacy. Students also need many experiences with other kinds of science language. Give them plenty of opportunities to read, write, label, and explain such science language as:

- cycles (e.g., carbon, water, moon, plant, energy, life)
- diagrams (e.g., solar system, plant parts, Earth structure, soil composition, DNA, atomic structure, molecules, body systems, mechanical processes, steps in an experiment, constellations, genetic combinations, cell structure)
- formulas and equations (chemical compounds, chemical reactions, finding variables such as *force, electrical energy,* or velocity)
- symbols
- signs (e.g., safety procedures, lab rules, how to use equipment)
- tables (e.g., periodic table, tide tables)
- graphs
- flow charts

SCIENCE VOCABULARY

GENERAL TERMINOLOGY

abstract	cause	constancy
accuracy	cause and effect	continuum
affect	change	contradict
analyze	chronological	control
anticipate	clarify	control group
apply	classify	controlling variables
approximate	components	correlate
array	composition	correspond
assess	conclusion	cumulative
bias	conditions	cycle
calculate	consequence	data
category	consistent	deduction

define operationally	focus	monitor
demonstrate	form	observe
dependent variable	form and function	occur
derive	formulate	oppose
diagram	fragment	order
differentiate	frequency	organism
diffusion	function	organization
digital microscope	gradient	pattern
discriminate	graph	perspective
distinguish	hypothesize	phenomena
diverse	identify	precision
domain	imply	preclude
dominate	independent variable	predict
effect	indicate	presume
electron microscope	infer	primary
elements	influence	principle
equilibrium	inquire	probability
equivalent	instance	probe
establish	integrate	procedure
estimate	interact	project
evaluate	internal	qualitative
event	interpret	quantify
evidence	introduce	reaction
evolution	investigate	reduce
exclude	isolate	relevant
exhibit	light microscope	representative
experiment	magnification	resolution
external	measure	results
extract	medium	scale
extrapolate	method	scientific law
factors	model	scientific method
features	modify	scientific notation

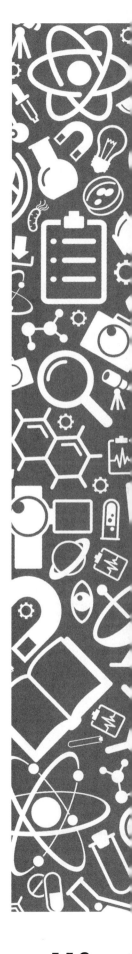

series

significant

source

statistics

structure

system

systematic

technology

theory

trait

transfer

variable

variation

vary

LIFE SCIENCE, Biology

aerobic

allele

alveolus

amphibian

anaerobic

analogous

anaphase

anatomy

antibody

antigen

artery

arthropod

asexual reproduction

ATP (adenosine
   triphosphate)

atrium

autonomic nervous system

autosome

axon

bacteria

bilateral symmetry

binomial nomenclature

blastula

blood pressure

body cavity

bone marrow

botany

brain stem

camouflage

capillary

carbohydrate

cardiac muscle

cardiovascular

cell

cell membrane

cell wall

cellular respiration

central nervous system

cerebellum

cerebrum

chlorophyll

chloroplast

chromosome

cilium

circulation

circulatory system

class

clone

connective tissue

cornea

cytokinesis

cytoplasm

cytoskeleton

dendrites

diaphragm

dichotomous keys

dicot

differentiation

digestive system

dioxyribose

disease

diversity

DNA (deoxyribonucleic
   acid)

DNA replication

dominant trait

double helix

ectoderm

embryo

endocrine system

endoderm

endoplasmic reticulum

enzyme

esophagus

eukaryote

evolution

exoskeleton

external reproduction

family

fertilization

fibrous root

fungi

gamete

gene

genetic characteristic

genetic code

genetic diversity

genetic engineering

genetics

genome

genotype

genus

germinate

gestation

gestation period

gland

glucose

glycosis

Golgi apparatus

gravitropism

herbivore

heredity

heterozygous

homologous

homozygous

hormone

host cell

hypothalamus

immune system

incubation

inherited traits

innate behavior

internal reproduction

interphase

intestines

invertebrate

involuntary muscle

iris

joint

kingdom

Krebs cycle

learned behavior

lens

life cycle

ligament

lipid

lymph

lysosome

mammal

meiosis

membranes

mesoderm

metabolism

metamorphosis

metaphase

microorganism

mitochondrion

mitosis

mollusk

moneran

monocot

motor neuron

multicellular organism

muscle tissue

muscular system

mutation

nerve

nervous system

neurons

neurotransmitter

nuclear membrane

nucleic acid

nucleotide

nucleus

offspring

order

organ

organelle

organism

osmosis

ovum

pathogen

pedigree

peripheral nervous system

phenotype

phloem	respiration	taproot
photosynthesis	respiratory system	taxonomy
phototropism	reticulum	telophase
phylum	retina	tendon
physiology	ribosome	thalamus
pigment	RNA (ribonucleic acid)	tissue
pistil	root	transpiration
placenta	sclera	transport
plant	seedling	tropism
pollen	sensory neuron	unicellular organism
prokaryote	sex chromosome	urinary system
prokaryotic cell	sex-linked trait	vaccine
prophase	sexual reproduction	vacuole
protein	skeletal muscle	valve
protein synthesis	skeletal system	vascular plant
protest	smooth muscle	vascular system
Punnett square	species	vein
pupil	spinal cord	ventricle
receptor	spore	vertebrate
recessive trait	stamen	vesicle
red blood cell	stigma	virus
reflex	stimulus-response	voluntary muscle
regeneration	stomata	xylem
reproduction	subspecies	zoology
reproductive system	synapse	zygote

LIFE SCIENCE, Ecology and Environment

abiotic factor	bacteria	biomass
acid rain	behavior	biome
adaptation	biodiversity	biotic
aggregation	biogeochemical cycles	camouflage

carbon cycle

carnivore

carrying capacity

classification

climate

colonial organism

commensalism

community

competitor

conservation

consume

consumer

decompose

decomposer

dispersion

diversity

dominance

dynamic equilibrium

ecological succession

ecology

ecosystems

endangered species

energy pyramid

energy transfer

environment

evolution

exponential growth

extinction

food chain

food web

genetic drift

genetic engineering

global warming

greenhouse effect

greenhouse gas

habitat

herbivore

heredity

hibernation

homeostasis

host

immunity

imprinting

inherited traits

instinct

interaction

limiting factor

microorganism

migration

mimicry

mutation

natural resource

natural selection

niche

nitrogen

nitrogen cycle

nonrenewable resource

nutrient

nutrient cycle

organism

oxygen

ozone

ozone layer

parasite

parasitism

pathogen

photosynthesis

pioneer species

point source pollution

pollution

population

population density

population dynamics

population model

predator

prey

primary consumer

primary succession

producer

recessive trait

recycling

renewable resource

resource

reusable resource

scavenger

secondary consumer

secondary succession

shelter

smog

specialization

speciation

species

succession

sustainable

symbiosis

water cycle

PHYSICAL SCIENCE, Chemistry

absolute temperature	coefficient	heterogeneous solution
absolute zero (third law of thermodynamics)	colloid	homogeneous solution
absorption	combustion	immiscible
acid	composition	independent variable
alkali	compound	indicator
amino acid	concentration	indirectly proportional
aqueous solution	condensation	inorganic compound
atom	conservation of mass	insoluble
atomic mass	density	intermolecular forces
atomic number	dependent variable	inversely proportional
atomic theory	diffraction	ion
Avogadro's Number	dilution	ionic bonding
balanced equations (mass conservation)	directly proportional	ionic compound
	distillation	isotope
base	electron	kelvin
boiling point	electron configuration	kinetic theory
bonding	electronegativity	law of conservation of matter
catalyst	elements	liquid
chemical bond	emulsion	mass
chemical change	endothermic	mass number
chemical compound	entropy	matter
chemical element	equilibrium	melting
chemical energy	evaporation	miscible
chemical equation	exothermic	mixture
chemical equations	families (on periodic table)	molar mass
chemical formulas	freezing point	molarity
chemical property	gas	molecule
chemical reaction	gas laws	neutralization
chemical symbol	graduated cylinder	neutron
	heat capacity	

Newton's three laws of
  motion
nonpolar bonding
organic compound
osmosis
oxidation
periodic table
periods (on periodic table)
permeability
pH (potential hydrogen)
physical change
physical property
polar covalent bonding

precipitate
principle of constant
  proportions
product
proportional
proton
pure substance
rate of reaction
reactant
reaction
reduction
resistance
salt

solid
solubility
soluble
solute
solvent
specific heat
suspension
transfer of energy
valence
vaporization
variable
viscosity

PHYSICAL SCIENCE, Physics

absolute zero
acceleration
action-reaction pair
air resistance
alpha particle
ampere
amplitude
angle of incidence
angle of reflection
angle of refraction
antenna
atom
atomic mass
atomic number
balanced forces
battery

beta particle
buoyancy
capacitor
Celsius temperature
  scale
centrifugal force
centripetal force
chain reaction
circuit
compression
concave lens
conduction
conductor
conservation of mass
consonance
constant velocity

convection
convection current
convex lens
crest
decibel
density
diffraction
displacement
dissonance
Doppler effect
Doppler shift
drag
dynamics
eddies
efficiency
effort force

electrical current

electrical energy

electrical field

electrical potential

electromagnet

electromagnetic force

electron

element

energy

energy transformation

equilibrium

focal length

focal point

force

frequency

friction

fulcrum

fuse

fusion

gamma particle

gas

gram

gravitational force

gravitational mass

half-life

heat

heat transfer
  (second law of
  thermodynamics)

hertz

incident wave

inclined plane

inertia

insulator

isotope

joule

Kelvin temperature scale

Kepler's laws

kilogram

kilowatt

kilowatt hour

kinetic energy

laser

law of conservation
    of energy (first law of
    thermodynamics)

law of reflection

law of universal gravitation

lens

lever

light

longitudinal waves

luminance

machine

magnetic

magnetic field

mass

mechanical advantage

mechanical motion

meter

momentum

movement

net force

Newton's first law

Newton's second law

Newton's third law

nuclear energy

nuclear fission

nuclear fusion

nuclear reaction

Ohm's law

Pascal's principle

photon

physics

pigment

pitch

potential energy

power

pressure

primary colors

projectile motion

projectiles

pulley

radiation

radioactive decay

rarefaction

ray

receiver

reflection

refraction

resistance

resonance

rolling friction

scalar

scientific notation

semiconductor

series circuit

SI (International System of Units/Le Système international d'unités)

sound

specific heat

spectrum

speed

superconductor

temperature

thermal energy

thermodynamics

thermometer

torque

trajectory

transformer

transparent

trough of a wave

ultraviolet

valence

vaporization

vector

velocity

visible light

volume

wavelength

weight

work

x ray

EARTH SCIENCE

ablation

abrasion

absolute age

absolute time

abyssal plain

acid rain

active coast

aftershock

air mass

air pressure

alluvial fan

altitude

aquifer

archipelago

arid

asthenosphere

atmosphere

atmospheric convection

atmospheric cycle

atoll

axis

bar

barometer

barometric pressure

barrier island

basalt

bathyal zone

big bang theory

biosphere

breakwater

cave

chemical weathering

cinder cone

cirque

cleavage

climate

climate change

coast

compression

condensation

continent

continental drift

continental shelf

contour currents

contour interval

contour line

convection

convection currents

convergent

convergent boundary

core

crater

crevasse

crust

crystal

cycle

delta

deposition

desertification

dew point

divergent

divergent boundary

drainage basin

drought

earthquake

earthquake focus

epicenter

epipelagic zone

equator

erosion

extrusive igneous rock

fault

fault line

flood

floodplain

fold

fossil

fossil fuel

fossil record

fracture

freeze

front

frost wedging

geochemical cycle

geologic time scale

geology

geosphere

geothermal energy

glacier

global warming

global winds

granite

gravitational effects

gravity

greenhouse effect

groundwater

gyre

half-life

hardness

high-pressure system

hotspots

humidity

hurricane

hydrologic cycle

hydrosphere

hygrometer

ice shelf

ice wedging

igneous rock

impermeable rock

infrared radiation

inner core

intrusive igneous rock

island

isthmus

jet stream

karst

kettle

landforms

latitude

lava

liquification

lithosphere

loess

longitude

longshore current

low-pressure system

luster

magma

magma chamber

magnetic pole

magnetic reversal

mantle

marine

mass movement

mechanical weathering

mesosphere

metamorphic rock

meteorologist

microclimate

mid-ocean ridge

mineral

Moh's scale

moraine

natural gas

natural resource

neap tides

nitrogen cycle

nonrenewable resource

ocean current

oceanic crust

ore

outcrop

outer core

oxbow

ozone

ozone depletion

ozone layer

Pangaea

passive coast plate
boundaries

period

permafrost

permeable rock

plain

plate

plate boundaries

plate tectonics

precipitation

pressure

psychrometer

radiant energy

radioactive decay

rain shadow

reef

relative dating

relative humidity

relative time

renewable resources

rift valley

rock

rock cycle

runoff

salinity

sand dune

saturation

sea floor spreading

sea stack

seamount

sediment

sedimentary rock

seismic wave

seismograph

seismology

shock waves

sinkhole

smog

soil composition

spring tides

stalactite

stalagmite

storm surge

stratosphere

stratum

streak

subduction zone

superposition

suspended load

thermal energy

thermocline

tide

topography

tornado

transverse wave

trench

troposphere

trough

tsunami

ultraviolet radiation

uniformitarianism

vent

volcano

water cycle

watershed

wavelength

weathering

wind energy

zone of aeration

zone of leaching

zone of saturation

SPACE SCIENCE

absolute magnitude

ampere

apparent magnitude

asteroid

asteroid belt

astronomical distance

astronomical unit

astronomy

axis of rotation

barometric pressure

big bang theory

black hole

carbon cycle

comet

constellation

convection zone

corona

cosmology

crater

crescent

diurnal tide

eclipse

elliptical

equator

equinox

evolution

expansion

galaxy

gas

gas giant

gravitation

gravitational force

gravity

impact

impact crater

light year

lithosphere

lunar cycle

lunar eclipse

lunar phases

magnitude

main sequence

meteor

meteorite

meteoroid

Milky Way (galaxy)

moon

moon phases

neap tide

nebula

neutron star

north pole

orbit

oscillating theory

outer planets

ozone

penumbra

photosphere

planet

prominence

protostar

pulsating theory

radiation zone

reflection

rotation

satellite

seasons

semidiurnal tide

solar eclipse

solar flare

solar mass

solar system

solar wind

solstice

south pole

space probe

space shuttle

spring tide

star

star cycle

sun

sunspots

telescope

terrestrial

terrestrial planet

tides

trajectory

umbra

universe

waning

waxing

ANSWER KEYS

Chapter 3, Variable? Or Unit? (page 91)

1. acceleration — V
2. amps — U
3. density — V
4. distance — V
5. energy — V
6. force — V
7. grams — U
8. gravity — V
9. heat — V
10. joules — U
11. mass — V
12. meters — U
13. momentum — V
14. newtons — U
15. ohms — U
16. potential energy — V
17. power — V
18. resistance — V
19. seconds — U
20. temperature — V
21. time — V
22. velocity — V
23. volts — V
24. volume — V
25. watts — U
26. work — V
27. specific heat — V
28. ΔT — V
29. pressure — V
30. λ — V
31. electric current — V
32. Ω — U
33. E_k — V

Chapter 3, Variable Match (page 92)

1. velocity
2. acceleration
3. p

4. potential energy
5. force
6. I
7. energy
8. ΔT
9. volts
10. density
11. Q
12. temperature
13. λ
14. resistance
15. time
16. E_k
17. c
18. gravity
19. distance
20. heat
21. volume
22. work
23. calorie
24. power

Chapter 3, Unit Match (page 93)
1. m/s
2. newtons
3. kg·m/s
4. joules
5. amps
6. Celsius
7. grams
8. watts
9. joules
10. seconds
11. Ω **and** ohms
12. volts
13. meters
14. g/mL
15. cm^3 **AND** mL
16. A **and** amps
17. joules
19. watts
19. m/s^2
20. joules

Chapter 3, Word Problem Strategies (pages 96 through 110)

1. Acceleration = Change in Velocity/Time $a = \Delta v/t$
   Change in Velocity = Acceleration x Time $\Delta v = at$
   Total Time = Change in Velocity/Acceleration $t = \Delta v/a$

2. Density = Mass/Volume $d = m/V$
   Mass = Density x Volume $m = dV$
   Volume = Mass/Density $V = m/d$

3. Electrical Energy = Power x Time $E = Pt$
   Power = Electrical Energy/Time $P = E/t$
   Time = Electrical Energy/Power $t = E/P$

4. Electrical Power = Current x Volts $P = VI$
   Current = Electrical Power/Volts $I = P/V$
   Volts = Electrical Power/Current $V = P/I$

5. Force = Mass x Acceleration $F = ma$
   Mass = Force/Acceleration $m = F/a$
   Acceleration = Force/Mass $a = F/m$

6. Heat = Mass x Specific Heat x Change in Temperature $Q = mc\Delta T$
   Mass = Heat/Specific Heat x Change in Temperature $m = Q/c\Delta T$
   Specific Heat = Heat/Mass x Change in Temperature $c = Q/m\Delta T$
   Change in Temperature = Heat/Mass x Specific Heat $\Delta T = Q/mc$

7. Kinetic Energy = ½ Mass x Velocity^2 $E_k = \frac{1}{2} mv^2$
   ½ Mass = Kinetic Energy/Velocity^2 $\frac{1}{2} m = E_k/v^2$
   Velocity^2 = Kinetic Energy/ ½ Mass $v^2 = E_k/\frac{1}{2} m$

8. Momentum = Mass x Velocity $p = mv$
   Mass = Momentum/Velocity $m = p/v$
   Velocity = Momentum/Mass $v = p/m$

9. Current = Volts/Resistance $I = V/R$
   Volts = Current x Resistance $V = I$
   Resistance = Volts/Current $R = V/R$

10. Potential Energy = Mass x g x Height $E_p = mgh$
    Mass = Potential Energy/g x Height $m = E_p/gh$
    g = Potential Energy/ Mass x Height $g = E_p/mh$
    Height = Potential Energy/ Mass x g $h = E_p/mg$

11. Power = Work x Time $P = Wt$
    Work = Power/Time $W = P/t$
    Time = Power/Work $t = P/W$

12. Speed (Velocity) = Distance/Time $v = d/t$
    Distance = Speed x Time $d = vt$
    Time = Distance/Speed $t = d/v$

13. Volume = Length x Width x Height $V = lwh$
    Length = Volume/Width x Height $l = V/wh$
    Width = Volume/Length x Height $w = V/lh$
    Height = Volume/Length x Width $h = V/lw$

14. Wave speed (Velocity) = Frequency x Wavelength (λ) $v = f\lambda$
    Frequency = Wave speed/Wavelength $f = v/\lambda$
    Wavelength = Wave speed/Frequency $\lambda = v/f$

15. Work = Force x Distance $W = fd$
    Force = Work/Distance $f = W/d$
    Distance = Work/Force $d = W/f$